Claiming your Kingdom

BREAKING THE SPELL OF INVISIBILITY

By Wendy Hammond

dp

COPYRIGHT

Dedication

TO T., T., AND B. I'M SO PROUD.

TABLE OF
CONTENTS

WELCOME

"The privilege of a lifetime is being who you are."

JOSEPH CAMPBELL

Once upon a time, there was a girl who had become a ghost in her own life. It was hard to say exactly when she lost herself. Giving up her career in lieu of her husband's made perfect sense when the children were young, as did the opportunities that followed to live in different cities and countries.

She remembers still being in possession of herself through the early moves and the excitement and the apprehensions – all were adventures. Roots pulled up, sails set. Dependencies were formed – so attractive at the time – because the company paid for the house, the school fees, the relocations. There... she can see how she moved away from her center. Giving over the rest of her power and identity was then only one step away. Doing so was slight, at first, deftly managed. Her faith and commitment to the marriage made the turbulence of changing dynamics a mere blip. It didn't matter. Not really. Not then.

Or so it seemed.

And so began her husband's late nights gone, and then early mornings. The swathes of time he spent traveling, until he was gone more than he was home. *It's for work*, she told herself – for that all-consuming job that makes everything else possible. Who is she to object? Aren't they so fortunate? A deluge of blessings so sharp as to cut the tongue.

Her husband went from partner to some form of pinstriped majesty, his heights loftier with every voice dubbing him "Sir." And that was the next step away from her center, a step more painful, but not tangible enough to make big accusations about. She licked her wounds and reminded herself of the great strain he was under, how hard he worked.

His job offered so many seductions for her, as well: travel, help with the children, their beautiful home. And so she made friends, took classes, bought things, planned dinner parties, and tried very hard not to burden anyone with the growing hollowness within. If she lived in a cage, well, it was so very well gilded that making any other choice would constitute huge losses and uncertainties.

And the numbing made that next, further step away from herself almost imperceptible.

At last – in a time far beyond her husband's original three-year contract – she had been away from her own career and home ties so long that they were mere dots on the horizon behind her. She had metabolized so many cultural shifts that she fit in everywhere and yet no longer belonged anywhere. Everything felt out of control. The pleasant expression on her face was the most fixed fragment of her world.

She looked around her life and realized that she owned nothing. She was the farthest tip of a tenuous link, attached to another tenuous link. Her husband's intellectual and physical needs were met elsewhere. She had become an optional side dish, an irrelevance. The marriage had devolved from a lifetime partnership into a repeating pattern of feeling pressured to prove her worth – which only seemed to underscore just how expendable she was in their ambition-fueled world, where absolutely everything, even the most intimate connections, could be bought. She felt an undertow of falseness and unsustainability running below it all.

She wondered how much longer it would be until she was marginalized, set aside altogether, completing her disappearance. She already felt invisible, powerless, ungrounded.

It would only take one more small step and she would be gone.

She took a look around and wondered if she was under a spell and whether it would be possible to still find her way back to meaning, mattering, and connection?

"I woke to find myself in a dark wood,

Where the right road was wholly lost and gone."

Dante

The Plight of the Trailing Spouse

This book is written for trailing spouses – perhaps, even more specifically, for expatriate trailing spouses – a population I know very well, having been one myself for 22 years. A *trailing spouse* is someone who follows their partner who moves for a job.

This book is also for women who have been carried away by their own careers or by mothering a special-needs child, or by caring for sick relatives. And for men carried away by their careers and commitments.

On a macro level, we're all trailing spouses in this world right now – with globalization and shifting changes of power taking place in all parts of the world.

The message of this book is that what is personal is also mythic, and what is mythic is also personal, and that myths, stories, and fairy tales can help us break the spells that restrain us.

The feeling of being adrift, rootless, and dependent on the employment – which is often fragile – of our partner is such a common plight of trailing spouses everywhere. The perks of the partner's job are often so good as to make us doubt ourselves, and keep us spinning in the same patterns.

The cons sneak up over time:

Lost sense of identity. It's easy to become a function in everyone else's life, rather than a player. After many moves, always playing the support role, and processing so many different influences and inputs, we can experience a temporary loss of a cohesive organizing principle, a guiding sense of identity.

Career compromise. Giving up jobs to support one partner's career means a cohesive career of one's own is compromised – often irrevocably.

Rootlessness. Expats know more than most that things are moveable and temporary. It takes time to build a network of friends, and they, in turn, tend to leave just as you've come to depend on them as confidantes and your children have come to depend on their own best friends. Those moves also tend to engender a sense of rootlessness, of futility in trying to build something like a business or long-term project.

Dependence on one's partner. Being at the mercy of one's partner – not only financially, but also perhaps in other ways – makes it difficult to mete out any meaningful consequences for relationship-damaging behavior.

Exposure to a wide range of cultures. There are many fabulous and fascinating things to see and learn around the world. And there are so many bits of other cultures that you may find disturbing. This is a con when the removal of the solid social constraints that you're used to results in developing weird expectations about what's okay and what's not, making you feel compromised on all fronts. You may find yourself living in areas of the world where, as a woman, you're prohibited from driving, or where the use of prostitutes is more accepted than you're used to, and that can be or feel undermining.

Monotype bubble. Within this expanse of the range of cultures you find yourself in, the expat community can feel very much like a monotype: Ambitious businessmen doing well in their careers, often at the expense of all else. If they get fired, they – and you – get sent home. If they get very sick, they go home. If they're not producing and succeeding they're sent home.

Overwhelm. Your Facebook life may look like a continuous rotation of parasols and peeled grapes. Okay, there are moments like that – but your life can also develop into a culture of "Keeping Up With The Joneses" – if you imagine the Joneses being jacked on speed and with an endless supply of fine whiskey, company yachts, and designer everything. The social engagements for the entire family, the school board you volunteer for, the children, your husband's job, the continual trips home with children, and what passes for "normal" living in a foreign country rain down such a mass of shifting details and demands that you are under constant threat of being washed away in the deluge.

The dark, cozy cloak of cash. In order to survive, you probably don't *need* to make a big change of your own, or make your own money, or expose yourself to the extent you'll need to in order to make that change. The fear stage of change can send you back easily, with a sharp kick, into the rut that welcomes you back with murmurs that you weren't really cut out for it, and that mediocrity is your milieu. *Here – have a gin and tonic and a cool compress for your head.*

Vulnerability. The house you live in, the school fees for the children that are often paid by the company, and lots of other perks – which are all only accessible to you through your relationship with your spouse. If the relationship turns bad, then everything you're leaning on begins falling away.

୬୨

But there are also so many good things:

Letting go of old patterns. Your lost sense of identity becomes a positive. A benefit of being an expat and trailing spouse is that the moves can function like a laboratory – providing space to start again, without the obvious ties to old patterns (making the internal ties all the more obvious and highlighted). Exposure to a different system and culture loosens our attachments to how we've always assumed things should be done, and makes us more flexible.

Self-reinvention. Giving up jobs to support your partner's career means you have an opportunity to reinvent yourself and to explore opportunities that you may not have had before. You get to reinvent yourself with each move.

Cultural exposure. Expats know more than most that things are moveable and temporary. When you are in places for a limited amount of time, you are most likely to take advantage of what is available in each place and gain a broadened view of the world and the different kinds of people in it. And you will have friends from different cultures and from all over the world.

Financial security. Even if your financial security is dependent on being with your spouse, it provides you with choice and opportunity.

ভ৵৶

How do we claim back a sense of our own power in this shifting landscape? How do we change our own lives when they are so intricately bound with another's in almost every way? How do we find meaning, when there are so many complex levels to our understanding of the world? *Within all that's out of our control, how do we take responsibility for our relationships and ourselves, our happiness, and our future?*

That is what this book and, indeed, the second half of life, is all about.

The Assumptions Made in This Book

In this book, I assume that you were born as more than a blank slate – that you have a personality and character that, at their very foundations, are comprised of more than the outer circumstances of your life's narrative. I also assume that there is not an inevitable culmination of a person that you are fated to become, but that you are a co-creator who can choose to continue living with the current defaults of your life that work, or choose another way and create a new default.

You were born with a purpose, a genius, and a mission uniquely your own, an inner pattern or story that calls you forward, a unique calling that will motivate you and tempt you forward with images and persistent pulls on your emotions and curiosity that defy the world's expectations and norms. This is your own particular quirkiness. It's what lights you up inside. It is that *thing* about you that behooves others to think of you every time they see an article or piece of artwork about that certain subject you love. What lights you up is much more than a hobby – it's a special way of seeing things that has followed you since childhood. It will press you forward, move you out of innocence and reticence, even when so doing makes you stand out. And following your special way of looking at the world will almost certainly make you stand out.

The path you are on in life is here to serve you. This includes every setback, betrayal, and wrong turn. One of the unhealthiest problems that has emerged from the culture of litigation is the continual seeking to lay blame on someone's shoulders. We stop seeing setbacks and challenges as opportunities and as inevitable issues that arise to be of service to our growth, and instead turn our energies to making sure we don't "lose out" on compensation for what we perceive as someone else's mistake; or, worse yet, to making sure we won't be held culpable.

What if, instead, we explored the notion that the challenges and twists and turns of life are pointers toward our purpose, rather than side-trips away from it? What if our wounds are part of the journey? More than that, what if they are the catalysts that activate the internally coded myth we are supposed to be living?

When we don't see our lives as the hero's journeys they are, but as a series of battles to win, we miss seeing the opportunities and possible solutions we're exposed to. We also start setting off chemical reactions that push us not into hero mode, but into depression and anxiety, so we start putting our energy into plastering over our supposed irredeemable cracks, building defenses and masks. Our energy would be better spent finding creative solutions to what's not right in our lives, questioning our fundamental assumptions, and looking for and sharing love.

What if our travels and the restless nature of the life we're living are an integral part of our destined myth?

It is part of your mission to find your own gravity, to become firmly rooted in your own identity, rather than casting about for signs and confirmation that you're okay, for explicit invitations to be in this world.

There is a path for you that leads to your own kingdom, however that looks for you. We've been given small clues throughout our lives that we can trace back and string together. Those clues – which take the form of memories and remarkable, numinous moments – can only be strung together in hindsight. It is in the second half of our lives that this work can be done. And it is when you are feeling the most lost that this task becomes not only intriguing, but necessary as well.

We live in a world with mountains and icebergs, toucans flying through steamy rainforest air, and manatees swimming through saltwater. Right now, all of these things are happening. Is it so hard to believe, then, that we, ourselves, exist on several levels at once? We are searching and being at the same time. We are searching for a way to be that feels more natural and alive.

You are sitting in a chair reading this book even as your soul wanders its world, looking for ways to make itself known.

Why Myths and Fairy Tales?

Social media and magazines claim that you can heal your anxiety in seven steps, or banish a lifelong habit in only a month. The honest truth is that big shifts take longer. Patterns of thinking can be broken in one session, but they re-form themselves into the same shape again soon afterwards unless we work with the subconscious mind as well, on a cognitive level.

If you have anxiety (and we all do, to a certain extent), there is no permanent cure without taking the time to reorient the foundations of your mindset. And even after that, the anxiety will hang around as a little bit of hyperawareness, waiting for an alarm signal.

Collectively, the onslaught of people and sources telling you that these dynamics can be resolved in "just a few easy steps" can eventually wear you down. You may begin believing that, because you have access to all of this information, it's only because of the stupidity, laziness, and a recalcitrant flaw within yourself that you are unable to carry through to the relief you seek, to stick to the clear regulations that will ensure your happiness.

But life continues to shift. And real change takes place at deeper levels. Every day brings a new challenge. Every year delivers a transformed situation. And they make your life better and more fulfilling, and/or more complicated and difficult.

This can all be pretty confusing. Distilled into a tagline, what I'm telling you in this section looks something like this:

"Life is really hard. And it's all for our benefit. Embrace it!"

"Oh, the beasts you will meet... some from within. Hurrah!"

Neither of those is very motivating. Our orderly and self-important egos want to insist that the situation can be knuckled under control with some mental elbow grease. Our rational mind insists that if we will only listen to its plans and justifications, all will go well. But that simply doesn't happen. Large changes in how we see each other and how we operate in the world are almost impossible to make using only the conscious, rational mind. We need to find a way to converse with the stronger, faster, and more powerful part of us, the subconscious self, which directs more of our behavior than we are often aware of or that we want to admit.

Myths and fairy tales give us a bridge between the outer world and our inner world of the subconscious. Myths are charged images, distillations shot through with meaning. What myths and fairy tales most grab your attention? This is different for different people. We each identify more with certain characters and situations.

Your subconscious mind – an unarticulated repository of your history, beliefs, fears, attitudes, automatic skills, and shadow aspects of repressed emotions – will try to keep you in the place it feels safest: in the patterns you've lived through since childhood. To do that, your subconscious will terrorize your mind with looped reels of worst-case scenarios. It will set anxieties loose, and haunt you as you're drifting off to sleep at night. It will lure you back into old patterns when you're feeling weakest.

The subconscious communicates in metaphor, images, symbols, emotions, sensations, and dreams. Synchronicities and coincidences have the fingerprints of the subconscious all over them.

Fairy tales and myths speak symbolically, so they're able to access the subconscious mind, moving past the firewalls of your defenses and attachments to the details of your angst.

Using fairy tales and myths therapeutically allows interaction between the subpersonalities of your psyche and the problems you are dealing with. And that allows an alchemical transformation to take place when creative imagination finds solutions and new combinations that make sense beyond what the logical and reasoning mind could construe.

Stories move us out of loops of thought. They extend our perspective, challenging the limits imposed on us. Stories communicate new possibilities and illustrate new perspectives. They can connect us to a new sense of meaning and purpose. Stories can illustrate patterns in characters that allow us to then recognize parallels in our own lives.

And they do so without patronizing us or judging us.

Fairy tales and myths have been handed down through centuries, surviving and adapting to society while maintaining their archetypes and messages. They weren't originally fashioned for children, but for sharing within the whole community, as reassurances that we are not alone, that the battles we face have been fought before and, in all honesty, that battles are unavoidable. One of my favorite quotes is, "Fairy tales are more than true – not because they tell us dragons exist, but because they tell us dragons can be beaten" (G. K. Chesterton).

The stories in this book have been sculpted to help you give your own subpersonalities and kinks a realm to live in, to help you productively interact with them, and to build your muscles, your confidence, and your peace of mind instead of depleting them.

I want to teach you another language for navigating change. This language shows you the steady rhythm of lush growth beneath the parched desert that can seem all-pervasive on the surface. Myths and fairy tales are a language full of examples of malleable and adaptive thinking, new paths out of paradox, real creativity, and deep change.

Fairy tales and myths give us heroic vision encoded with emotion and magic. They help us see ourselves through to the other side – into our own kingdom.

The Language of the Subconscious Realm

The stories in this book will likely awaken the archetypes within you. Keep your senses open to receive them. It can be helpful to keep a journal as you read this book, so you can record the dreams you have and the synchronicities you notice. Remember that the language of the subconscious realm is images, metaphor, dreams, and synchronicities.

Sink into the experience of the stories, and into your own sensuality. We're letting the rational brain take a well-needed rest here. *Feel* into these stories, and let sensuality open doorways into the wisdom your body wants to share. Although these stories are old and have been passed down through the ages and told to millions, the sensations you feel as you experience them are absolutely your own. Practice feeling them, savoring them, and accepting that those sensations are personal messages, just for you. Our senses inform us, pleasure us, warn us, and encourage us to move on or dig deep. They allow us to drop out of the relentlessly rational world that eventually deadens us to our purpose and our soul if we never look away.

What is your story? What myth are you currently living? What complexes and archetypes are active in your life? Are they helpful? Or are they holding you back? Are you lost? What's keeping you from finding your way? Do you know where your soul is taking you? Are you dragging your feet because you think the calling you feel is certainly too large and too loud for one such as yourself to embody?

Throughout the book, we will look further into how to interpret your very specific stories that come up as you read the stories told here.

"Unfold your own myth."

Rumi

Going Forward

It is time to ignite your soul, that incandescent place within you that is personal and yet also mythic. Finding connection with the depths and powers within you is a great adventure. As with all adventures, there are risks involved and there are frightening challenges. There may be failure and heartbreak and letting go, but the gains will be of mythic proportions, too.

By the end of this book I hope you have a better idea of the mythic journey you are personally on, to the point where you've gotten in touch with:

The villains and the vanquishers in your psyche.

The frogs waiting to be princes.

The make-up of your own personal interior castle.

The strong woman.

The wise woman.

The flow.

The quest. The quest. The quest. Your wounds are urging you to go there.

Your genie wants out of the bottle.

Chapter 1

THE FROG PRINCE AND FAITHFUL HENRY

You may be surprised to hear that in the original stories of the Frog Prince, the princess did not achieve frog-to-prince conversion by way of a kiss. On the surface this is a story of a spoiled and careless princess, an uppity frog, and an absurdly stern king. Looked at symbolically, we find a princess growing into a queen, an emerging subconscious and the reclaiming of a whole self.

The Frog and the Golden Ball

Once upon a time there lived a princess who loved nothing better than to play with her golden ball. When things in the palace became too dull for words, she would take her golden ball out into the forest and play by the well – tossing and then catching the shining gilded orb. One fateful afternoon, the golden ball failed to land solidly into her hand and fell straight into the dark water of the well with a loud glug. Though the princess thought she could just make out a golden glint from within the depths of the well, it was far too deep for her to reach. She began to cry, first in delicate whimpers, then escalating rapidly into sobs fit to shake leaves from the trees.

"Why are you crying, lovely princess? Your sobs could make a stone feel pity."

The princess stopped mid-wail to see who was speaking to her. "Oh, it's you, you old splasher," she said to the frog who had settled into a patch of weeds beside her. "I'm crying for my beautiful golden ball, which has fallen into the well."

"Don't worry. I can help you," offered the frog. "But what will you give me in return if I retrieve your ball from the bottom of the well?"

"Oh frog! I'll give you anything you wish! These pearls, my jewels, this velvet dress, even the crown upon my head. My golden ball means more to me than anything else in the world."

The frog hopped a bit closer. "Your pearls, your jewels, your dress, your crown mean nothing to me – but to have you as my closest friend would be heaven. We could play together, live together, eat from the same plate, share the same bed. For that I would gladly return your golden ball to you."

The princess held back a gag as she considered the proposition before her. What a silly, repugnant little creature, she thought to herself. He lives in the forest and sleeps in the mud. We could never be friends. He doesn't realize what he's saying. I really want my ball back though. "Yes, frog. If you rescue my golden ball from the bottom of the well, I promise to be your best friend."

Without a moment's hesitation the frog hopped into the well. Whorls and bubbles played across the surface of the water, rippling the reflection of trees and sky. Just as the princess's patience was wearing thin with waiting, the frog emerged holding her golden ball proudly in his webbed palms. "Here you are my friend."

The princess scooped up the ball and held it close to her heart. "Thank you frog! I'm terribly grateful!" Off she ran through *the trees, faster than any frog's legs could keep pace with. She gave one rueful glance back as she reached the edge of the forest. Though she felt bad about her ruse, the frog really had asked too much. She shuddered at the thought of sharing a plate or a bed with such a cold, clammy little beast.*

Precious Things and Slimy Accommodation

This story begins with a princess tossing around her golden ball next to a deep well. Gold symbolizes the eternal divine self, the part of us that is not only our adapted social self, but the wholeness of who we were born to be. The symbolism of the orb, the circle, the ball symbolizes living in the unity of our masculine and feminine sides.

Ancient cultures, and many today as well, believed we are each born with a specific genius, or *daimon* – a template of who we are meant to be. This is different from a *fate* that we have no say in. Fatalism is saying, "Today I wake and eat an apple for breakfast because that was written in the stars before I was even born." With fatalism there is no choice. A genius, or daimon, is more of a guiding principle – a spirit or angel who hovers nearby with eyes and heart looking for the experiences that will open our souls. It's the part of us that lights up when something specifically meaningful to our soul is nearby.

When we look back on our lives, it is not like we are watching moment-by-moment footage of each step, each sip of a drink, each individual interaction that occurred. Instead, we remember powerful vignettes. Moments that wounded, healed, thrilled, or frightened us.

Moments that were meaningful.

What is it in us that paints some memories as worth remembering? Our own personal soul has a hand in this. There are some moments that are universally compelling – our first kiss, our first heartbreak, leaving home for the first time. But others are subtler, more mysterious in their ability to persevere in our minds and hearts. Even within a close family, interpretations of a single event differ from one person to the next. After their parents's divorce, their son may remember the split being painful and see it as having long-lasting negative effects, whereas their daughter may remember it as having been a blessing, and that it went smoothly and was handled well by her parents.

When we are very young, before we learn what is acceptable and what is not in the family and society in which we live, before we begin labeling experiences, people, and thoughts as *good* or *bad* – our daimon is readily available. We are free to follow our delight, to screw up our faces and balk at that which doesn't appeal to us. Slowly, though, we are enculturated and these behaviors are tempered so as to not be a complete nuisance to everyone around us. We change to fit in with our society. Our survival as children depends on this. In order to abide by the rules – some of which are very useful and some of which involve a clipping of wings that we could do without – we form a provisional personality.

The task in the first halves of our lives is to put down roots in our world and our culture, to make our place, build a network of connections and a family, establish an income, learn how to operate in our community.

During this enculturation, however, our golden ball – our wholeness – becomes obscured, little by little. A part of it dulls when we are told that we must share our toys with our new little brother, which we do with a smile on our face. We are told, at some point, that running around naked in the sprinklers "at your age" causes everyone embarrassment. And so it goes, until the day we toss our slowly disappearing golden ball into the air, expecting it to land back in our outstretched hand, only to discover that it has disappeared altogether. So much has been concealed within our subconscious that we can now no longer reach it, though the glimmers of it reach the surface of our consciousness every so often – reminding us of what we have lost.

Our wholeness includes the parts of us that others turn their eyes away from. Their doing so teaches us to feel ashamed, as well – ashamed of our natural anger, our sexual instincts, our tendency to eat all the cake or to stroke a stranger's arms. Clearly, even the most libertarian of us will understand that enculturation has its place. Who wants to live among a population of overgrown two-year-olds?

Losing touch with the golden ball is a part of life.

As we get busy with the tasks of the first halves of our lives, we think of the diminishment of our golden ball very little.

We accept the yoke of society – more or less – seeing it as comfortable and necessary. Until the day comes when we have achieved the tasks set before us and the absence of our wholeness begins to hurt. When we've turned over so much of ourselves to our roles – wife, mother, help-mate, PTA leader – that we have become a shell rather than a real, living, breathing being. We're lost and we feel the need to pull back into our sense of wholeness. We want to feel meaning again, to emerge from the inertia and sense of loss, anxiety, and depression that has crept up and that now clings to our arms and legs wherever we go.

Forests and deep pools of water represent the subconscious realms of our being. The subconscious is the unarticulated repository of our repressed emotions, fears, automatic skills, and the shadow aspects of the parts of us we deny and that our communities wish to look away from. And here in this story we find a princess in the woods, near a deep well. She is a young, feminine character whose ball, her wholeness, has just disappeared down in the murky depths of the sub-conscious.

Because this is a fairy tale it's much leaner and more honest than a "real life" story. The loss of the princess's golden ball is felt deeply and grieved immediately. We could say that her innocence has been broken. Who knew that who she was could be lost? Is it really possible that that which we are – that intangible part of ourselves that cannot be stolen from bedside tables or accidentally left behind in a restaurant – can be lost?

Where and when did you lose your golden ball? Consider the steps that led you bit by bit away from yourself to this spot where you stand by the well catching only glimmers of that shine?

The princess must face her inadequacies and realize that she will be unable to retrieve the golden ball herself. It has fallen deep into the subconscious and she will need assistance to retrieve it. She is immature – a princess still and not yet a queen. Her ways of being in the world are not yet established, but are still in development.

It takes the loss of the golden ball – that opening up of ourselves to learning about loss and darkness – to become the queen. Queens represent the established modes of valuation and intuition. A queen would not be tossing her golden ball above a well. A queen would recognize the value and the danger of such a game. But queens were also once princesses.

༄

Down there, in the depths, the golden ball is spending time with the shadow aspects, recovering the wholeness that our sunlit world of cultural expectations had shut away, and picking up the energy (one might even say the majesty) of the shadow, the underneath places.

There is a whole network of intelligence under the surfaces we see. Mushrooms dotting the forest floor share roots that spread and communicate for miles around. Tree roots reach down and intermingle with minerals and spring water and grubs and burrowing animals. A whole ecosystem of life exists below the surface.

It is the same with us. Below the surface of our social personalities, our false smiles and pain, lies sadness, but also the answers that we have lost access to.

The painful recognition of what the loss of the golden ball means – the loss of our wholeness and the recognition that we will need to get it back by means heretofore untried and potentially underhanded – is the first intimation of real adulthood. But the crossing over to psychological adulthood can happen at any age, and may even need to happen more than once. Some people cross over during deep pain in their early 30s, and some do not cross until their 60s. The crossing is almost always catalyzed by pain – the pain of loss of meaning, the loss of a marriage, a child, a job, a parent – anything that turns the world upside down. Illnesses can do it, or financial ruin. It would be a rare thing indeed to rise from sitting in a sunny patch on a warm day, set down your lemonade, and stand up to declare that you have decided to change your life entirely.

Luckily, life has a way of helping us along. Sometimes with a painful wallop, sometimes with a hollow slump, we hit a new place when we deeply question, asking, "Is this really all there is?" Our provisional personality has just met the end of its solo road. It needs to deepen to make space for the whole of you. The second half of life, it could be said, is all about getting connected with peculiar, eccentric, quite specific (and even awkward) *you*.

And so appears the frog. Frogs can bridge subconscious and conscious lives: breathing the air of our sunlit world or oxygen in through their skin while diving to the depths, even going into a deep sleep until the circumstances are right for their emergence. Archetypally they are associated with fertility (they spawn hundreds of eggs at once) and transformation (they change from jelly-egg to tadpole to legs-sprouting until, finally, they become a frog).

From the depths of our subconscious, this frog comes laden with the stickiness and mud of the shadow – what we don't want to acknowledge about ourselves. But also, with the power to bring back our wholeness, our golden ball, which is vital to our destiny and to finding meaning in our lives.

This is why the princess, a girl enculturated into her royal family – the ultimate in established modes of being – is so repulsed by the insistent offerings of this creature still sticky from the silt of the underworld. She knows she wants her golden orb back, and is willing to pay dearly for it – offering her jewels, her gown, even her crown. This frog is no dummy, though. He knows what's really at stake. And he is seeking his own wholeness.

Please keep in mind that each of the characters and important objects in myths and fairy tale stories are the entirety of who we are. We are the frog as well as the lost golden ball. We are the princess as well as the king sitting on his throne back at the palace.

The frog knows that if he returns the princess's ball and lets her go on her way without suitable payment, perhaps only minus a pearl or two, the dynamics of the kingdom will stay the same and will eventually wind down into the inertia of rule only by the established society.

The subconscious realm is always seeking a way to be lived.

What about you? What discomforts and yearnings does your subconscious regularly prod you with as it searches to bring your whole self into balance? Do you have repeating thoughts? Are there dramas in your life that play out repeatedly? What are the elements of those dramas that hook you each time? What subconscious element, emotion, or message is trying to emerge? What are those dramas trying to bring into wholeness?

If your mind came up with answers that made you flinch a bit, it's likely you've hit on something you've disowned in yourself that may be trying to have a voice in your life.

In that moment of being willing to negotiate for the retrieval of her golden ball, in service to reclaiming her wholeness, the princess is willing to consider allowing a door to the shadow side be opened – despite her repugnance. She is no random Barbie doll, after all. She knows that her golden ball is not replaceable. We're given one for life, and its loss will keep us suffering its absence forever. It is only the reclaiming of it that will bring back meaning and purpose to our lives.

This story, this reclamation, is about resuscitating what we've considered our negative instincts, those we had pushed into the shadow. We need to resurrect them in order to live as fully as we need to, in order to be whole, in order to act honestly when we share. What is being asked is that all our instincts are given a seat at our table, that we become able to recognize them in ourselves and make the choice as to how much we will let those suppressed instincts come to the surface and live in our lives. Perhaps we are not willing at all, though we know they are there. Perhaps there are some that we readily readopt into our daily lives.

The point is to *recognize* those deeper instincts in ourselves, to acknowledge our range of aspects, our ability to be kind and generous *and* to place limits on those qualities when our boundaries are being crossed; to be able to intellectually make rational decisions *and* to know that rationality must be augmented, or even overthrown entirely, on occasion, in favor of the interests of our hearts and for the betterment of humanity. This is not merely an exercise in serving ourselves. This process of accepting what's beneath the surface is what keeps us truly connected to the world around us. When we do this, we develop compassion and are better able to communicate with others and know where they are coming from. What we gain is our own protection and delight.

And so the princess makes a promise that she has no true intention of keeping. In this, we see the shadow aspects emerging already. Though we may blame our subconscious elements for surprising us – with a sudden wave of vocal anger or jealousy – we also make promises to our shadow aspects. We let them out, but then turn our faces away. We want people to know we are fierce enough to defend our opinions – but then we swallow down our conflictive rebuttals time and again. In doing so, we again turn our normally sublimated emotions and selves into the unwanted, the uninvited guest, the outsider, the unloved. Another favorite quote of mine is, "You must be proud, bold, pleasant, resolute, / And now and then stab, when occasion serves" (Christopher Marlowe).

So the princess promises this amphibious member of the kingdom that they will be the best of friends – if he will just do this one thing. She doesn't want to forge a relationship with something as unrefined as a frog. *What would the neighbors say?!* The frog retrieves the ball, which the princess takes, and then she rushes off faster than the frog can keep up with – back to the castle and her established way of life.

But she underestimates the reach and commitment of the subconscious aspects, the frog, to have a place at the table. She believes that distancing herself will be the end of the story. She's wrong, as we shall see.

Amphibious Persistence and Rigid Rules

Amid the chatter of dinner that evening at the castle, there came a knock at the palace doors. The doorman entered the dining hall to announce that a frog had arrived, and this amphibious visitor insisted on seeing the princess.

The princess rolled her eyes and groaned.

"What is this about?" asked the king.

"My golden ball fell in the well this afternoon and the local frog offered to pull it out for me. He made me promise to be his best friend and allow him to live here in the palace with me. It is absurd."

The king knit his brows together and looked closely at his daughter. "Did you promise the frog this thing? Did you agree to this?"

"Well, yes. But I never thought he would actually show up here at the palace and seriously expect to be let in. He's a frog. He belongs in the well."

The king set his fork down firmly on the table. "You are a member of the royal household. If you made a promise, then it is a promise you must abide by."

"You can't be serious. Father. This is a frog we're talking about."

"Nevertheless, a promise is a promise.'" The king nodded to the doorman. "Bring our new friend in. He has been pledged a place at our table."

All those dining fell into an aghast silence at the kind's proclamation, so the splotch splotch splotch of the frog's damp approach could be clearly heard. All eyes, with the exception of the princess's, strained to see the frog as he entered the room.

Hopeful, the frog hopped until he reached the princess's chair. "Princess, pray tell why you left me behind in the forest today after I rescued your ball?"

The princess sat stonily, her eyes fixed on a small section of the table's wood grain.

"No matter," croaked the frog. "I'm here now and we will be the best of friends. What's for dinner? I'm quite famished after my long journey to the palace."

The princess allowed one pea to roll off the edge of the table and land next to the green creature.

"Princess, my dearest, we are to share a plate. This is no way to treat your soulmate. Lift me up so we may dine from the same dish and drink from the same goblet."

The king called for the footman to place the frog upon the table. The guests began eating again, pretending it was quite an ordinary thing to have a talking frog sharing dinner from the princess's gilded plate.

With one webbed palm, the frog held a grape up generously toward the princess's mouth. She turned away. He maneuvered her golden spoon aside so he could sip from her soup *bowl. She turned all her attention to spreading butter on her bread.*

Finally, dinner was done and the princess stood to return to her bedroom in hope of forgetting all about this terrible day.

"Princess! Don't forget me! We are to share a room and greet each new day together. Remember your promise?"

The princess turned back to the table, an outraged look on her face, which the king met with a glare of his own. "A promise is a promise," he boomed. "Your friend here looks as though he will need a hand up the stairs. Treat him well, for he is a guest in our palace."

"I am a princess and this is a frog," she declared. "A frog. A damp, squidgy, wart-ridden beast who was sleeping in the mud last night and ate flies for breakfast."

"There's no need to get personal," croaked the frog.

"A promise is a promise, daughter," insisted the king.

And so the princess lifted the frog by one spindly leg and carried him, ingloriously, up the stairs.

The Doorway in the World's Great Wall of Rules

Undeterred, the frog makes the long journey to the palace. The frog and our daimons are persistent. They are the parts of us that we insist on not recognizing, that we deny, and that have the most power over us. We will never see their machinations if we never look at them. Instead, we fall prey to the worst-case scenarios. We're afraid to look at our finances, so we look the other way, until the money is all gone and we have no choice but to sort things out. The problems in a relationship are so onerous to sort that we get very busy at work, until the day we come home and discover that our partner has left.

Take a look at your own life. What persists in your life, no matter how fast or how far you run? The daimon is persistent there. It is not particularly reasonable or understanding of protocol or conventions or previous entanglements and commitments. That's why the daimon is not a great fan of innocence or unquestioningly following along with or adhering to rules.

The king, hearing the frog's story, is rigid in his expectation that a promise made is a promise that must be kept. Certainly this is an important lesson to embrace as one matures. If we do not honor the commitments we make, the consequences are mistrust from those around us. The princess is walking a difficult line between being true to herself and seriously disregarding herself and getting into a lifetime relationship with an amphibian. At least, that is how it appears on the surface.

Archetypally, the image of a king denotes the established masculine attributes in the story – and in ourselves. Kings symbolize rationality, fixed meanings, structure, and logic. They want to *think* their way through every situation in life, and maintaining the status quo is of utmost importance. In myths and fairy tales, the characters are the symbols, so this is a king symbolizing that a promise made must be kept – even if that means marrying a frog.

The frog is persistent. Our daimons are persistent. The voice of our inner soul will keep whispering, keep pushing – and it is inevitable that when the established way of being and the deeper yearnings eventually knock together there will be a shattering, and a breaking away toward new ideas and new ways of being.

Note that there is no queen currently at the table. A queen symbolizes established feminine attributes. Whether we are a woman or a man, to live a balanced life in this world we need to incorporate both the masculine and feminine sides of our psyches in order to live a healthy, meaningful life. The feminine aspects encompass desire, imagination, subjectivity, and feeling. In this story, the absence of a queen denotes the absence of a valuing, intuitive perspective. It is likely that a queen at the table would ameliorate the inflexible dictum of the king and take into consideration the spirit of the rule, rather than only an unbending adherence to it.

But that is not the point of this story. The absence of the queen means that this is a story calling out for the mature feminine to fill that gap. Otherwise the balance of the whole story universe is broken. In the same way, the absence of an established feminine side in our lives can make us feel lost.

A queen is the seat of wisdom, but wisdom is more than intelligence and more than knowledge. Wisdom is worldly knowledge mixed in with a feeling-sense of how things are. Wisdom cannot exist in the one-sided brightness and experiential ignorance of a princess. To become a queen – a mature woman in possession of her own powers – the wholeness of existence needs to be brought in. That means that the princess needs to widen her world, and so the golden ball – her daimon – needs to spend time in the dark shadow world. Only upon its recovery will she, and do we, mature and become whole enough to claim the throne.

Because she's a princess and not a queen, the choices allowed in the princess's life are conditional and depend on the approval of the king. Clearly, cracks in this dynamic are beginning to show. The princess defied the dictums of the kingdom privately, but the king brought her back into alignment with established ways. Now the real test is at hand. Will she be able to stand by her own convictions, even though this whole predicament was pretty much her own fault? One accident plus a white lie, and suddenly she's got a frog as a soulmate.

A "good girl" would suck it up. Okay, she might secretly hate every moment and marinate in resentment for the rest of her life, but she could always claim it was never her fault – she was just doing what was expected of her. That's quite a trade-off, isn't it?

Why is it important to cultivate our own identity and will, even when it's difficult and goes against the established way things are? If we don't, we are at the mercy of others's whims and often untrue projections of how we should live our lives. In all honesty, we are faced with this pressure whether we are in touch with our center or not. But if you are not *moored* to yourself, you will find yourself racing to keep up with every voice insisting they know best. Without a solid sense of self, we fall victim to narcissists and sociopaths and people with strong, judgmental opinions. Without honoring our own intuition and wisdom, our connection to our daimon becomes lost, and then we, in turn, feel lost and are unable to access our own precious anchor. We lose the connection with our soul. When that happens, we cannot offer to others – like our children – what we have not yet developed in ourselves.

When we don't show up with our own golden ball in hand, we become mere reflections. We become side salads at the banquet rather than the main dish we are intended to be. Side salads are only interesting for so long. When we lose our center, serving anyone is hard. The loss of a marriage or job turns us into rudderless shrapnel. Not knowing how to prioritize, what to let go of, what to hang on to, is a sure recipe for depression and anxiety.

The loss of one's daimon will throw relationships into chaos as well. Golden balls keep relationships interesting. They give surprises and anticipation a place.

The Prince and Faithful Henry

The princess's bedroom was at the top of the stairs. Once inside her room, she cast the frog into a heap of spare cushions in the corner of the room. "I'm sure you shall be most comfortable there. Do not breathe too loudly and don't move around much, because I am a light sleeper. I really think you'd be much more at home in a room of your own. Are you sure we can't set you up somewhere else? The moat looks particularly cozy in the moonlight." Her eyes drifted toward the window and she prayed for the frog to remember his familiar comforts of swamp and silt.

The frog was undeterred. "Your silk sheets look fine to me. And your bed seems quite perfect."

"That is out of the question, frog." The princess began brushing out her hair, her cheeks flaming in repressed fury.

The frog dragged a floor cushion closer to the bed, which was no small task for his size and web-bound limbs.

When it was clear that she would not be able to don her nightgown without his bulgy eyes observing her, the princess stepped into her closet to change, growing ever more annoyed with each inconvenience.

She emerged from the closet to see that the frog had used the cushion as a stepping stone from which to hop onto her bed. There he lay, frog arms behind his frog head, plump, pale belly exposed like a miniature rotunda. He emitted a low, rhythmic ribbit sound.

The princess's face grew hot. "This is not to be borne, you slimy green freak! I am grateful for your kindness, but you ask too much. Get out of my bed immediately!"

The frog sat up. "But you promised. You promised. If you do not let me sleep in your bed with you, I will tell your father." With those words, the princess whisked the impertinent frog off her bed and threw him with all her might against the wall.

By the time his body landed on the floor, he was no longer a frog, but a handsome prince with beautiful, kind eyes.

The princess was stunned to silence.

The prince laughed as he shook out his arms, spreading and bending his fingers and standing up to his full height for the first time in years. "Ah, thank you, princess, for breaking that old spell." He looked at her kindly and told her how he had been bewitched by a wicked witch. If she had not broken the curse he would have remained a frog forever.

The princess blinked at him for a few minutes, until the shock began to wear off. Where moments before a fire of rage had been burning in her chest, there now glowed a warm and open heat radiating through her whole body. She sat on the bed and motioned for this beautiful prince to sit next to her.

The prince and the princess talked well into the night. Near dawn, they pledged to marry and travel to his kingdom.

The king rejoiced at the news and welcomed the prince as a husband for his daughter. He sent messengers to alert the former-frog-prince's kingdom of the good news.

One morning, soon after the messages had been dispatched, the princess and prince awoke and were informed over breakfast that a large, golden carriage drawn by eight white horses decorated with white ostrich plumes on their heads was waiting at the front gates. On the back of the carriage stood a serving man with three iron bands secured around his chest. So great had been his grief when his master had been turned into a frog that he had asked a blacksmith to fashion the bands around his chest to keep his heart from breaking.

"My faithful Henry!" called the prince as he rushed to embrace his good and loyal friend. After happy introductions, Henry helped the princess and the prince into the carriage and took his place behind them.

They had only driven a short distance when a sharp crack startled the couple. "What was that, Henry?" the prince asked. "Is it the carriage breaking?"

"No sire. All is well," Henry returned.

A little further down the road another loud crack was heard, and again the prince asked if the carriage was holding up. He was again assured that all was well.

When a third sharp crack rocked the carriage, the prince turned to see his faithful Henry crying tears of joy. Though the bands around his heart had been forged in grief, joy had made them burst. The cracking sounds had been the bands around Henry's heart breaking open and falling away.

Enchantments Crushed and Freedom Found

We bargain with our shadow selves. *Okay, then, I'll admit that I have angry and ungenerous thoughts, but they must sit over in the corner. Or, better yet, wouldn't they be better off going back in my subconscious?*

We become mired, caught, as the frog was caught, in a spell, stuck in place waiting for something to break the spell. It is often someone else's anger, crushing the comfort of our acquiescence, that does this. It's painful, but ultimately enlarging. Or we spend our lives chasing the high of pleasing others.

The frog went from the well deep in the forest to the threshold of the castle to the dinner table, where the king insisted he be allowed into the princess's bedroom. Each step allowed the frog deeper and closer access to the princess's privacy and personal space. Bedrooms are where we can, in many ways, leave the world's demands behind and concentrate on healing ourselves from the day's indignities. Where we can come back to ourselves. They are often the place where we allow ourselves to surrender to sleep, to be at our most vulnerable. A bedroom is an intimate space where we rest and renew ourselves. It is where we dream and, in so doing, converse with our subconscious. On the surface, this is the most disruptive space for an uninvited other to breach. If looked at archetypally, however, it is the perfect place to engage with the frog as an insistent source of the subconscious trying to come through.

Little by little, the frog insinuates himself – right into the princess's bed. He continually battles her wishes – holding over her the power of the king's words, the status quo, and doing so over and over to overrule her feelings, her repugnance, and her choices. The princess relents, little by little, by making concessions. First she conceded that he could sleep in her room, but insisted not in her bed. Then she went elsewhere to change, as the frog wasn't budging. Little by little, her boundaries are tested and she gives in on the small things.

But the small things add up.

How does this play out in your life? What compromises have you made and then made again? Have others in your life met you halfway as well, by making compromises of their own? Or are the compromises primarily yours – a continual erosion of what is important to you without a balance from the other people in your close relationships?

Finally, the frog crosses the line. When the princess emerges from the bathroom, he is lying in her bed, right where she had repeatedly forbidden him to go. Her anger finally gets the best of her and she breaks the hold of her father's word and her own restraint and throws the frog against the wall.

Why would throwing the frog against the wall have such a delightful effect of turning him into a prince? Firstly – a threshold has definitively been passed. The bargaining has stopped and an actual decision has been made by the princess to let go of the ties that bound her to having her most intimate space and attention be continually encroached upon.

That splat against the wall was a wake-up call for the frog-prince. Now that the princess took a firm stand, the spell is broken and he can be the gentleman. He's now in a form that she can take seriously and have an actual relationship with. An equal relationship. She showed up. She owned her feelings and made her feelings and their consequences quite clear.

It is only when we show up as ourselves that we can be loved as ourselves. Otherwise we are only masks admiring masks. It is being visible and not hiding behind roles and conventions that allows intimacy and wholeness. I'm not suggesting that you begin throwing around all of your frustrations and frog-like companions. I am asking you what setting boundaries and being yourself would look like in your life.

When we do things – even risky, awkward, scary things – in service to our soul's voice we feel an immediate energy flow, a resonance. Even if we didn't do that thing as perfectly as we'd hoped, or that thing we're doing hasn't (yet) reached the heights of success, we envisioned, the *doing* of it feels good, even within the frisson of uncertainty and newness.

We're looking to build a better biography – a richer, expanded version of ourselves to take us into true adulthood – and a beautiful relationship with ourselves, where our souls are given expression, where the person we were called to be here on this earth in this time has space and voice to bring us into blossom.

This process of finding your kingdom is about blowing away meaninglessness, giving safe harbor to feelings of right destiny, and becoming your essential self, in addition to your enculturated social self. Deepening. Brightening.

Who was that wicked witch who cast the spell on the prince and made him a frog? Why did she do it? Perhaps, as part of the human condition, we will always, of necessity, take the path of change, turn with the wheel of life. It can feel like a curse though. "Growth experiences" rarely arrive through massage or ice cream cones.

The princess and the prince can now come together – to marry in fairy tale terms. And we now have a mature, new male character and a matured female character who are almost ready to claim their own kingdom. When the prince's faithful servant arrives, with great fanfare, to pick them up, the great bands around his heart burst open with the joy of this – the promise of a new kingdom.

Journal Prompts

Who is served by you holding on to the principles that keep you stuck in place? Under what conditions would those holds be releasable?

What is persistent in your life, no matter how fast or how far you run?

What eyes do you see things with? Does everything that happens to you seem like fodder for a book, or do you see colors and characteristics of light that you can bring out in a painting, or are you aware of different possibilities for how to market a business?

Artsy Sensory Prompt

Make a vision board. Put together images that touch you and make you feel good. Let your body and senses choose the images, rather than your mind. Never question why. Once you've made it, put the board where you can see it when you wake and before you go to sleep.

Geek Fact

Some interpretations of this story theorize that the frog represents male genitalia, and the frog's transformation into a prince represents the sexual maturation of a new wife overcoming her disgust for the sexual act.

Chapter 2

ADAM, EVE, AND THE GARDEN OF EDEN

In the story of the Frog Prince we looked at the loss and reemergence of the golden ball, a symbol for our soul – the wholeness of who we are, of the joy and sense of meaning that comes when we are in touch with the wholeness and calling of who we are. Holding that sense of wholeness is like finding your home within yourself. Inner shifts in attitude and outlook that now have space to happen will call you to make outer changes, to become more visible. The first steps here are often the hardest.

Internally, this feels right – but the world we've built around us is often reluctant to share in the joy. The pushback – loving or otherwise – from our families, partners, and friends can feel like reproach and we may feel shame. Our emerging self often seems threatening to the status quo that keeps those around us feeling safe.

So, how do you go about living your truth, your soul into the world? This is a chapter that honors the difficulties and the courage of this important quest, as we are taking responsibility, setting our own boundaries, and moving forward.

This quest means leaving the walled garden of certainty and childhood and walking into the world a vulnerable woman. We often try to buoy ourselves up by building elaborate justifications about our decisions, looking to avoid blame altogether, or making our choices as bulletproof to others as possible. That is another form of keeping ourselves encapsulated in a walled garden built not by our own hands and heart.

How about letting go of unnatural ideas of perfection – which are always someone else's standards?

Would it feel right if the most the world could say of you was that you were irreproachably acquiescent? Or do you want something better for yourself?

Life in the Garden

There was once a divine garden created by God. This Eden was filled with many kinds of living things. Within its tall walls you could catch glimpses of golden sunlight glinting off the four streams that flowed through, the glow of spotted fur charging past, and beautiful feathered beings flying from tree to tree.

In the very center of the garden stood the Tree of Knowledge of Good and Evil.

From the clay of the earth, God made the first man, Adam, and put him in Eden. God told Adam that he could eat any of the fruit he liked, except the fruit of the Tree of Knowledge. God then set Adam the task of naming the animals – and so the furred beasts became lions and leopards and horses. The feathered beings became hummingbirds and cardinals and jays. All were beautiful, but none were equal to or similar enough to be a partner quite right for Adam.

God sent Adam into a deep sleep and took one of his ribs to make a partner for him – Eve – so that Adam would not be alone. Together, Adam and Eve walked naked and happy through Eden, at peace with themselves and with God.

It was perfection.

Gardens and Walls

Gardens are so alive, verdant, fruitful… and cultivated. This story does not take place in the wilds. Rather, like in a castle or an established kingdom, the elements within are chosen or ruled out. Weeds are pulled up, and forces (like peckish deer or hungry beetles) are guarded against. This is a space where a greater force – the author's version of God, in this case – has made choices that made the environment for the inhabitants who come after. Yet, unlike castles, gardens call in the life force of the earth. We can choose to plant hydrangea bushes in our gardens, but the exact angle at which the branches will twist, and which day the blossoms will bloom, are out of our control. Depending on the pH level of the soil, the flowers could bloom pink, blue, or purple – so we make choices about how far our choices will go.

Gardens depend on rain, or a very diligent waterer, in order to survive. And on the sun, the minerals in the earth, and winds that aren't too wild. In a garden, there is a combination of choices made and natural growth. Rather like in our own lives.

The garden in this story is walled and protected, with one tree standing at the center –the Tree of Knowledge of Good and Evil.

God reaches down and forms man out of clay, the very substance that makes up the soil of earth. It's malleable, which means it can be formed into any shape, and then can be reformed as well. Within the Bible and in a host of older creation stories (such as *Gilgamesh* and earlier stories), we find living beings formed from clay. We are, as humans of this earth, the same – ashes to ashes, dust to dust. We begin as earth, and will one day return to it. But, for the duration of our lives, we embody an animated spirit.

Adam is thus born and, in an action that sets him apart from the other living creatures in the garden, he is asked to name them. They are each seen from his particular perspective. For all we know, the ibex prefers to be known as a Pfeffernuss. What we are being called to see here is the forming of a world called *Adam*. As he names the creatures, his intellectual perceptions set him apart as a singular creature, with a singular perspective, and singular powers. As such, he finds himself alone, without a partner of similar stature.

When Adam has been slipped into subconsciousness, God uses his rib to form Eve, his companion, and, for a time, they are happy and content with themselves, each other, and the garden as created by God. Eden is the only world they have ever known. In this way, Eden is very similar to childhood.

Whatever environment a child is born into is all he or she knows for quite some time. What the baby sees simply *is. This is my mother. This is myself.* The room they live in is *The World*. Mom with her quirky purple hair and tendency to make tweeting sounds while watering her plants: The World. It is only as we are exposed to more and different people, perspectives, places, and situations that we begin discerning ourselves from others and realizing that our circumstances are only one continually shifting fusion in an endless multitude of possibilities. Within The World, our Eden, values are presented to us as though they are universally accepted – inevitable culminations of wisdom and globally tested treatises of good and ill.

As long as we are accepted and our physical needs are seen to, this sheltered and fully acceptant world is very cozy. There are no life-altering decisions that lay in our hands. Lines and boundaries are clear. We are free to play and learn and take in experience and information. The experience and information that is available in this cultivated, enclosed garden is ideally safe and uniform, but is ultimately static. This stasis is what makes Eden and perfection so easily destabilized. One might even say desecrated.

Snakes and Temptation

One day, as Eve was wandering through the gardens, the lithe and devious serpent dangled down from a branch to whisper in her ear.

"So, tell me, beautiful Eve, are you allowed to eat from every tree in this Garden of Eden?"

Turning to the snake with a sweet smile, Eve answered, "We may eat the fruit of any of the trees in this garden, with the exception of the Tree of Knowledge in the middle of the garden. God has said that if we eat or touch it we will die."

"Oh pish," intoned the snake with a tilt of its head. "You will not die if you eat the fruit from the Tree of Knowledge. You will come to know the difference between good and evil, and become godlike yourself. This is why God has forbidden you this fruit, so that you will not be as a god."

A shadow passed over Eve's normally unmarked brow and she looked curiously from the snake's dark eyes to the fruit hanging from the central tree's branches. The apples were at their peak – round and red and ripe. Ready to be eaten. Eve yearned to taste of the fruit and the promise of its wisdom. She was beginning to question, because she was sensing a limitation where before she saw the Tree and God's rule about it as only a matter of safety.

The snake nudged the heavy fruit with its tail, causing it to twirl a little on the branch. A small buzzing began in Eve's mind. She reached out to feel the firm, cool apple and found herself grasping the full solidity of the fruit, hearing the snap as it came free from the branch. She held its smooth skin to her cheek before biting into its tart, sweet flesh. The apple from this tree was unlike anything she had tasted before. As the juice ran slightly down her chin she realized she wanted Adam to share the experience with her, or else it would sink into secrecy, as though it had never happened. Wandering into the grove where Adam was, she passed the apple to him and he ate from it as well.

At that point, they looked at each other and became aware of their nakedness and became ashamed. They sewed together fig leaves to cover themselves.

Snakes and Apples

Serpents, snakes – there is such a global wealth of symbolism that snakes embody.

Firstly, they are a symbol of renewal and transformation. They shed their skin on a regular basis, leaving the dried husk behind. For both snakes and ourselves, our skin is what we show the world. It also gives us all sorts of information. It tells us what temperature the air is, if there is a wind blowing, if someone's touch feels pleasurable or painful, how much pressure is being exerted either upon us or from us. It stores wounds in the way of scars and it also self-heals. Skin has different textures. It has calluses where it is most used, and is so soft in other, more protected places. It freckles and tans and reflects our cultural lineage. It stretches and changes tremendously as we grow. It is a personal barrier that protects us from the outer world, that keeps us contained and separate.

As snakes begin to shed their skin, the eyes form a milky white film. This, too, will be shed with the rest of the skin. It is as though they are periodically moving into a whole new way of seeing, and refreshed ways of sensing input and the environment.

What would our lives be like if we, too, could so regularly and ordinarily peel away old ways of seeing and doing things, without feeling like we needed to justify it to ourselves and to all those around us?

Snakes are also associated with wisdom and healing. The caduceus – a staff upon which two serpents are entwined – is the modern symbol for medicine and doctors.

The sight of snakes is also one of the few instinctive fears that we are born with, most likely because of the range of poisonous and deadly snakes found all around the world. Snakes are fast. They can be unpredictable. As they are cold-blooded, their body temperature depends greatly on external influences and, because of this, they will brumate during the winter to conserve their energy. Brumation is similar to hibernation. They will burrow underground until the temperature warms up. They do not entirely go unconscious and, even on a sunny December day, they can come back up to the surface to sun themselves on rocks.

We can see that – like the golden ball that spent time down in the well – snakes spend time underground as well.

Snakes have been considered a symbol of the sexual and creative life, which, in turn, connects to and represents regeneration.

Here in our Eden is a snake tempting Eve to eat from the Tree of Knowledge. The snake explains that it is not mortal death which will ensue upon the consumption of the tree's fruit – though the snake does not mention the psychological dissolution that will occur once the awareness of paradox, opposites, and moral reasoning ensues upon gaining a subjective sense of right and wrong and all the shades in between. In many ways, the words of the Creator set up the first duality. By saying, "Do not eat the fruit from this one tree," he directed attention to that tree.

The day we perceive ourselves as separate – as beings *in* the Garden of Eden, rather than being the Garden of Eden ourselves – is the day we realize that there is a larger and more varied world beyond our doorstep and our mindset. It is at this point that we need to make a decision about whether to become a part of the larger, more challenging, world, or turn our focus and energies to continuing the endless and impossible maintenance of the perfection of Eden, which would now involve shielding our eyes and intellect from influences beyond those that have been spoon-fed to us by whichever culture or household we were born into.

Maintaining Eden is no drift on a summer's breeze. Seeds must be removed from the plants and kept dry. Even one raindrop or a kiss of dew invites an opening, a blossoming, an awakening of roots to reach deep into the soil and shoots to stretch toward the sun, and that's dangerous because the only things allowed are what have always been allowed. Not wildness.

Keeping good and evil separate means no dance. No intercourse. No coming to understand. No acceptance. No new growth.

We learn so much that's good from our families of origin, and it is our place in the world to let those excellent lessons – the ones that sing to our souls and empower our hearts – sink down into our bones and give us strength and bearing. Inevitably, however, well-meant insights will be passed on that clang loudly and discordantly within us. And these we must question and release, or weave into something that makes sense to our transforming soul and the ever-evolving world around us. In the words of Ken Wilber, a transpersonal psychologist, to grow we must continually transcend and include. That doesn't mean turning our backs on all that our families and even ourselves have held as truths up to now. It does mean expanding our vision in a way that allows space for new information and experience to augment what exists already.

Eve chooses to eat the apple, which initiates a change from unquestioning unity with the rules of Eden to questioning and separation. Eating the apple is a choice of knowledge over innocence; independent thinking over dependent mimicry and extended infantilization. To stay the seed but never become the fruit means we never bear fruit. Something in Eve's soul knew it was time to expand. So she makes the choice to eat the apple.

Or does she?

Was she free to defy or ignore or condemn the snake? From such a place of innocence, it is difficult to determine where personal culpability ends. It is from experience that we learn about and hone our ability to discern. It is only from experience that we embody knowledge rather than juggle abstract theories about the world at large.

Think about your own life. What does it feel like to know something intellectually versus knowing something through experience? Think of a situation or circumstance in which you had an intellectual conceptualization before you experienced it for yourself. How was the reality, the experience of it, different from your preconceived idea of how it would be? How is being a parent different from the idea you had of how being a parent would be? How is drinking a glass of wine different from abstract calculations of what drinking a glass of wine is like?

How is the actual taste, texture, and juiciness of an apple different from the thought of or someone else's description of eating an apple? Whether she did it by free choice or divine inevitability, Eve ate from the apple.

Let's look at the symbol of the apple. Like the golden ball in our previous story, the apple's roundness depicts a sense of wholeness. Within its round shape lay the seeds of new life. The ensuing generations from this one apple alone could spawn an orchard, in time. It is a ripe fruit – the culmination of a seed, sunlight, minerals from the earth, rain from the heavens. It is mature – no longer a bud or a blossom. It is ripe. It will quench hunger. It is food – that which we take within our bodies to be metabolized into energy which we expend on action, thus taking its energy within us and then sending it out into the world.

The skin of the apple is red – a color often associated with passion, anger, and lust; the color of blood and fire; the color of the base chakra, which has to do with existence and survival. Alchemists called the last stage of turning base metals into gold *rubedo*. It was the reddening of the brew, and the last stage before completion of the alchemical objective – transmutation into gold.

When Eve had eaten from the apple, she looked to Adam to share the experience. Together, both having eaten from the forbidden fruit, both having metabolized moral freedom – the freedom to choose, the ability to question and go against the stated rules – they felt suddenly naked and vulnerable. Their differences were apparent. That discomfort led immediately to the wish to cover up, to revert to the established mode of life where there was no discomfort of uncertainty.

But it is too late. They cannot go back to unknowing. A threshold has been crossed.

Consequences and Release into a Bigger World

Soon Adam and Eve could hear the Lord God walking in the garden. They fearfully attempted to hide themselves, but God called out to Adam. God asked of him why he had been hiding and Adam replied that he was afraid. Through Adam's admission, God immediately knew that the forbidden fruit had been eaten.

"Why have you disobeyed me in this way, Adam?"

This is when a whole lot of finger-pointing began taking place. Adam pointed out that it was Eve who had fed him the fruit. Eve explained that it was the serpent who had deceived and tempted her.

God's displeasure was not to be appeased by the passing on of blame.

God cursed the snake and banished Adam and Eve from the garden. From that day forward, the whole of snakedom would crawl on its stomach as the lowliest of all creatures. And, henceforth, the entirety of mankind would live by the sweat of his brow and womankind would suffer the pains of childbirth. Where there was once eternal life, mankind and womankind would experience death.

East of Eden was a cherubim with a flaming sword who was stationed to guard the garden and so also guard outside access to the Tree of Life. Adam and Eve passed by the cherubim and were thus exiled from the Garden of Eden.

Consequences and Exile

The consequences of Eve's action brought the creator's wrath down upon her head and Adam's. With moral freedom comes moral responsibility. Crossing into adulthood, leaving our cloak of invisibility, entails taking responsibility. This means being vulnerable and admitting our fallibility.

As adults, we make tough choices in an uncertain and ever-changing world where right and wrong is rarely clearcut, where actions that will ensure life in one area may end life in another. We make the choice to take one job, which entails closing the door on another possible future, one that was also neither all good nor all bad.

Keep in mind that this is a garden – a renewing, living entity, with seasons of growth, harvest, fallow, and budding. Without the ripening and harvesting or the death of one season's growth, there would be no room for the next season's buds to emerge. The ever-renewing cycle of life would be held captive, dead in its stasis, because life is dynamic and encompassing of death, as well as the animation we call *life*.

Trying to maintain innocence is the stunting, binding, and freezing of that healthy movement. Naïvety is a fool's glory. You become easily manipulated, penned in, controlled. To stay the seed, but never become the fruit means we – and our lives – never bear fruit.

There is a part of us that is forever reaching for newness, toward consciousness, in this world. It is the feminine aspect within us that pushes, so it is not surprising that it is Eve in this story who reaches for and bites into the apple. Remember that this is not about being female or being male. Each of us has these two aspects within us: our outward-focused, active part – the masculine side; and our part that gathers wisdom, that is valuing, and that internally chooses – the feminine side.

Biting that apple was the crossing of a threshold that could never be undone. Once we see the dualities present in the world, once we accept paradox and the fact that life exists on a spectrum, that our characteristics exist on a spectrum, that we, naturally, embody them all, then we own our choices, even if they are against social mores.

Descent, initiation, and the crossing of a threshold feels like exile. We can no longer believe, eat, or see only the flat and one-sided dimensions of the world we once thought was the entirety of life. Leaving the garden means accepting and submitting to growth and uncertainty. We will transform, but we cannot be sure where these transformations will take us, or what will take place within us. We are annealing ourselves, creating resilience and depth. We are transforming.

Crossing the threshold allows a release of energy, and that allows the power of our shadow aspects to emerge. We begin to learn how to rein them in and mold them into empowered, but not reckless and undermining, forces.

Broken is hoping for some kind person to take pity on you in your wretchedness. Broken is victim mode. *Transforming* is feeling a pulse, knowing your potential is there. Transforming is knowing you are on a quest.

Perfectionism is the slimmest of tightropes – a standard that is always changing. It is reductive, narrow-focused, "other than," emptily aspirational, clipping, domesticating, following, derivative, prefabricated, and other-defined. It keeps your locus of evaluation always external. Perfection means there is a standard by which to judge against, but different people have different belief systems and standards; therefore, perfection is an ever-moving target.

Questing, on the other hand, is transformational, annealing, strengthening, growing wiser and more discerning, expansive, open, noticing, resourceful, adventurous, forging, creative, self-referred. Questing comes from an internal locus of evaluation.

Give up on being perfect and begin the work of becoming yourself. Allow your heart to be pierced. There are a thousand ways to heal it.

The sword is a symbol for discriminating consciousness. The gates of Eden – that place of undifferentiated consciousness – will now be guarded by swords. The gates are set in the East, where new beginnings appear with the rising sun.

Once we leave the walled garden, we enter a world with a cacophony of influences and images and passionately held opinions that are often at odds with our own. This is why it is so important to be in touch with your soul, with your own valuation system and sense of whether or not something is right for you intact. Try to leave behind the elusive certainty that because it is right for you it is right for everyone. We are individuals living in a community made up of people with a brilliant array of skills, talents, and backgrounds. We are all here for us to complement each other – together. Not for us to impose on others, but to find a cooperative way to co-exist, co-create, and love. And be challenged by and grow from these challenges.

But we must stick our head above the parapet to enter into life.

Seeing challenges and difficulties as punishments is childish. It is the mindset of an immature psyche that believes all elements in the world work together in tandem, that there are universal rules and regulations governing each step. Life may even feel safer that way. But it is not true.

Consequences are to be moved through, changed by, embraced.

A fall from grace is a fall from innocence into the evolutionary reality of life, where our decisions and actions carve our way forward and help to prepare the way for the generations coming after us. Not with the hope that they will follow our personal dictums to the letter, but that they will take our world and make it their own in their time for their own wholeness.

Wholeness is birthed by struggle. Conflict helps us hone our own opinions – experienced rather than merely theoretical opinions. We can tell our minds anything until we experience the issue firsthand. We hone our opinions and our lives by following always the song, the sound of our soul's overarching *yes*; by following the senses and the kinesthetic *yes* within us, those hints of freedom, release, and liberty.

Perfectionism is a way to keep you in the garden, and your kingdom is not inside that garden. Staying in the garden, in innocence, secluded, is a very personal fanaticism that keeps us from questing.

A garden can be perfect because it's the creation of one psyche. But this world is about relationship. We are all in this together. There is no perfection because there is always more than one psyche at work. We can try to completely subsume ourselves to the insistences of another, but we will only find balance within ourselves. From there, we find balance with others.

ভ৵৶

In the next chapter, we'll follow the trail of a prince who is absolutely unable to stay in his cage of perfectionism – and his life fares all the better for it.

But, first, I'll end this chapter with an excerpt from "Song of the Open Road" by Walt Whitman, which I feel embodies the spirit of leaving Eden:

From this hour I ordain myself loos'd of limits and imaginary lines,

Going where I list, my own master total and absolute,

Listening to others, considering well what they say,

Pausing, searching, receiving, contemplating,

Gently, but with undeniable will, divesting myself of the holds that would hold me.

I inhale great draughts of space,

The east and the west are mine, and the north and the south are mine.

I am larger, better than I thought, I did not know I held so much goodness.

Journal Prompts

Why would we choose to stay inside the garden gates? For safety, blamelessness, comfortable invisibility?

What are the benefits of leaving the garden?

If you were to cultivate your own garden, what would you include? What would you leave out?

Do you claim perfectionism as a facet of your nature? Perfectionism is often a defense we feel we need to deploy to make up for a fault we imagine ourselves to have. "I have to keep my house perfectly clean to make up for being unsuccessful." Or lazy. Or stupid. Or...? What is your perfectionism covering for?

Visual and Sensory Prompt

Make an aerial view map of the "garden" you grew up in. Include the important elements within the garden, but also include what lies beyond the walls.

Geek Facts

Some versions of this story say there were two trees in the center of the Garden of Eden – the Tree of Knowledge and the Tree of Life – and it was only after the fruit of the Tree of Knowledge was eaten that the Tree of Life could be seen.

Sources of this story from Jewish folklore depict the snake as the demonized embodiment of Lilith, from the Bible – the first woman. She refused to be subservient to Adam and was banished from Eden before Eve was made from Adam's rib.

Chapter 3

THE PRINCE, THE FOX, AND THE BLUE FEATHER

Once we have sensed the call of our soul and tuned in to it, how do we give it voice in the world? A change in attitude will make the lasting and sustainable change of behavior possible. This isn't to say that, once attitudes have changed, the behavioral changes are inevitable. Justification and mental reframing is faster and less fixed than committed action. Changes in behavior require conscious commitment over time and the public redefining of ourselves in our own minds as well as in the minds of others.

This is all about becoming visible.

When an internal shift is expressed in our outer lives, we are no longer able to blend in as we did before, hiding seditious thoughts behind politeness and stoicism. So, how can we handle these new and more meaningful narratives of possibility, especially when flashes of a more meaningful life – one that entices but is not yet being lived – run through our awareness like a blue falcon gliding in and out of the tree line?

This Celtic folktale of The Prince, the Fox, and the Blue Feather tells of a prince mercilessly harassed by his wicked stepmother and his awkward journey toward resolution, with invaluable assistance from a talking fox, and the eventual claiming of his kingdom, a beautiful new queen by his side. Looked at symbolically, this story is about evolving our way in the world, spurred along by changing our inner attitudes. It is a journey of many revolutions that lead, step by mysterious step, to reclaiming wholeness and the ability to live the myth we were called to bring forth into the world.

Princes, Blue Feathers, Wicked Stepmothers, and a Quest

Once upon a time there lived a king of the Scottish Isles who had one son, Prince Iain, who was strong and fast and shot an arrow as straight and as far as the best Scottish marksmen. The king had recently married a new and sly queen who spent much time plotting how to be rid of the prince. One day, she saw her chance.

After a day of hunting, the prince came home empty-handed except for a feather fallen from a magical Blue Falcon.

"Have you brought nothing to our table today?" asked Prince Iain's stepmother.

When he took the blue feather from his bag, his stepmother snatched it from his hand and used its powerful magic to cast a spell upon him: "From this day until the one in which you bring me the bird this feather fell from, you will wander the world with a puddle in your shoe, cold and filthy. Let it be done!"

Prince Iain had his own knowledge of magic and he wheeled on her in his already dampening shoes and shouted, "Until my return, your one foot will stand on this castle and your other on the barn. You shall suffer every drop of rain that pummels down in that spot and every cold wind that races through."

The prince set off immediately to find the Blue Falcon, leaving his stepmother in a much colder and wetter predicament than his puddle-bound shoes.

Discomfort in the Soul and the Start of a Quest

Here we have a prince with a father who does not appear in person in the story, and a mother who has died. Princes, as we discussed in the Frog Prince story chapter, represent the emerging masculine. They are new ways to live in the outer world, not established and throned, but seeking and adventuring, trying new things. Princes are often seen kissing sleeping princesses or slaying dragons. This one, however, is still hanging about his father's castle, despite the death of his mother – the established inner feminine. A shift has taken place internally in this kingdom and where there was once a loving status quo, we have what appears to be a malevolent feminine force lodged in what was once a comfortable castle and family. For us, symbolically, the castle is our established way of life.

With the reign of a new queen, an internal shift has taken place within the prince's established life. She is his stepmother – inferring strangeness. Though she has taken residence, the prince does not know her or speak her language.

Intuitive shifts happen automatically within our psyches as we are exposed to wider worlds and different points of view. Through experience, we begin recognizing the misconceptions, anomalies, and failures inherent in our assumptions (castle). Our old paradigms get battered and replaced by new intuitive forces we don't explicitly understand. We find ourselves yearning for ineffable change and forms of ourselves we cannot find from within our current approaches to life.

This is what drives the prince from his home after his unsuccessful hunting trip: the search for something nourishing, some food on the table. For us, that's something tangible to feed our souls. There is nothing in the prince's old, outmoded kingdom except the flash of a blue falcon. Prince Iain aims his arrow, but misses – gathering only a blue feather to take home.

In general, the symbology of birds speaks to a connection with a higher, spiritual realm. Falcons have the ability to fly very high. They see ultraviolet light and their migrations span 18,000 miles as they travel from different climates – from Siberia to South Africa. Those qualities speak especially to the ability to draw on divergent and broad forms of living information.

Falcon images have been used to represent a "celestial eye" – they signify a protector of pharaohs in Egypt, and they were carved onto graves to ensure the rebirth of the pharaoh – the transformation of matter into spirit and again into matter. Falcons represent visionary power, and focus.

The feather dropped to the prince is blue – another message from the spiritual realm. Blue denotes transcendence and the beyond. Blue is the color of vast skies and seas that exceed the human condition. The feather's connection is transpersonal, connecting the prince to a consciousness previously unknown. The blue feather has magic within it, and the changing internal consciousness – the stepmother – sees this immediately.

Of course, it's just a feather that was brought down by the prince's arrow aimed at the falcon. But this feather is like an urging from the universe for our response. It is very likely that at the first sign of our bigger soul waiting for us to step into it, we are not quite ready. It is by struggling through misdirection, trial and error, and course correction that we finally find our way. We often do not know where following a feather, a spiritual stirring, is going to take us. And that's where the discomfort comes in. In this story, the catalyst for the discomfort is the new queen. For us, it is usually our mindset, our own personal internal valuing system that is trying to expand against the boundaries set by an older paradigm.

The new queen curses the prince with continual, distracting discomfort. This shows up for us as internal shifts that no longer allow us to carry on in jobs that have become meaningless or in relationships which have become hollow and destructive, without experiencing ever-present malaise. It may be pain we think we can bear, but we will never be able to ignore. In some ways, bearable pain can ultimately prove more diminishing than acute difficulties, because it feels more comfortable than going through the intense anguish of putting ourselves out into the world. So many people and groups carry on in the space of uncomfortable malaise instead of forging ahead and out into a new place that feels better.

The new queen wants not only a disconnected feather of spiritual connection; she wants an alive and robust relationship. She wants the falcon. She wants to cage it within the castle – if it can be done. Because the new queen is an archetype for an evolving feminine subconscious, not an actual woman, she needs the prince – that masculine external energy – in order to take action toward maturation. Only through engagement can we transform. This is the dance within each of us, male or female, between our masculine and feminine energies.

Though a king is mentioned in this story, note his absence. There is no mature masculine energy to balance the restless, destructive feminine here. Things in this castle are out of balance.

Just as the prince from our Celtic tale would surely have survived (fairy tale princes are immune to hypothermia) if he did nothing to break his stepmother's spell, so would we if we stayed on our set course. The curse in the prince's case is water in his shoes. Though it will not strike him dead, he will not spend another day comfortably unless he follows the impetus to change. Unless he follows that feather, there will be no peace.

As frustration and distress build, we begin to find ourselves becoming disenchanted. Although it is more comfortable to ignore the call to adventure, that blue feather, doing so can lead to neuroses, addictions, depression, anxiety, and physical illness. We live in the safest and most affluent society known in history, yet we are also the most anxious and depressed society ever known. Perhaps this is because we perceive we have so much to lose.

And so the prince is set upon his path. The hero's journey begins. As he wanders into the woods, so do we need to leave our well-worn paths in order to find the falcon to our feather. The prince's hunting forays have previously been confined to his father's grounds. He has not yet learned the art of discerning his own way. We need to learn new external approaches, as well as the language our subconscious speaks, if we are to forge a new life more in line with our soul.

Everything in the story world is connected – just as our own different levels of consciousness are connected. As the queen has cursed the prince, so also will she need to bear the exposure and discomfort of the prince's quest.

When we head out into the woods – our subconscious – to develop ourselves further and to bring our voice into the world, uncertainty will buffet and blow at us from all directions.

The Forest, a Fox, and a Five-Headed Giant

The prince walked out beyond the castle grounds, out into and through wasteland and wilderness, looking for the Blue Falcon. As night fell, he was still empty-handed. He prepared to spend the night alone beneath a prickly briar bush, resting his head on the gnarled roots.

After a while, when dark had almost fallen, Gillie Martin the Fox came along and laughed heartily at the prince's dilemma. "You're the picture of misery this evening, Prince Iain. All I have to eat is a sheep's leg and jaw, but I'll share what I have with you."

They lit a fire and roasted the meager meal and slept soundly amongst the roots of the briar bush. In the morning, Gillie Martin offered the prince this advice: "The Blue Falcon you seek belongs to the Brutish Giant with Five Heads. I'll show you where he lives. Go to him and tell him you can care for his swine, cattle, goats, and sheep. Tell him your specialty is birds and you can take care of his. In time, he may trust you enough to care for the Blue Falcon. When this happens, treat her well, and then, when the giant is not home, carry her out gently, taking care not to let a single feather touch anything in the giant's house."

"I'll take care," promised Iain. He slept fitfully and the next day made his way to the giant's castle, where he plucked up the courage to knock on the door of the Brutish Giant with Five Heads, and knock he did.

"Who's there?!" bellowed the giant from a window high in the castle, his five large, angry heads straining to see who dared come to his door.

"I'm a farmhand and bird-keeper, sir," Iain shouted up. "I've come looking for work!"

The heads pulled themselves indoors and a loud, tumbling rumble could be heard as the giant descended the stairs, until, finally, the Brutish Giant with Five Heads was standing in front of Iain. Some of his heads looked dubious; some looked hopeful. The giant hired the boy and set him to work caring for the many animals and birds on his estate. Over time, the giant saw how well Iain cared for the livestock and how gently he handled the birds. "This boy is good enough to entrust the feeding of my Blue Falcon to, I believe," the giant said to himself one day, and he showed Iain how he wanted the feeding to be done.

As the fox had suggested, Iain waited until the Brutish Giant with Five Heads was away and then carefully took the Blue Falcon out of its cage and cradled it under his arm to carry it away. As they neared the door, with the great wide sky beyond it, the Blue Falcon spread its wings to take flight and her feathers whisked against the doorway. The doorway let out a loud screech! and the Brutish Giant came running home to secure back the Blue Falcon.

Though Iain was scared of what the giant might do, he managed to ask what it would take to have the falcon.

The giant said, "You may have my falcon only if you will bring me the White Sword of Light from the Seven Big Women of Jura."

Over-Intellectualizing and Discernment

We start this part of the story with Prince Iain going out into the wilderness, really not certain of where he needs to go to look for this Blue Falcon. He's just wandering, waiting for some sign, which never comes. At night he lies down on the roots of a bush.

All of these elements – the wilderness, the night, the roots that reach down into the deep ground – symbolize the subconscious. We have left the castle – our known way of doing things – and are descending into the part of ourselves that can make fundamental changes. We've left our boundaries, our castle walls, behind, but have not yet made a home somewhere else. This is an exciting, but also an anxiety-making, place to be.

Boundaries, virtues, and roles may be limiting, but they are also reassuring. When there are rules – and we know what they are – we can play by them and know that we are safe and will be accepted. When the boundaries crumble, the resulting sense of openness can make us feel very vulnerable.

It is in this liminal, in-between, place that we find foxes. The fox symbolizes the force inside us that begins to soften up the principles and make us more flexible, and serves as a bridge that allows the shadow sides of us to come up closer to the surface and be seen.

The woods are dark and the way is unclear, and so the prince needs a guide – and one appears in the form of a sly fox. Foxes rest in burrows underground, but hunt above. The fox is a trickster who is equally comfortable in the woods and shadow as in our backyards and consciousness. He has an instinctive cleverness that is not of the rational world, but is close to it. Foxes form a bridge between the subconscious and conscious elements of ourselves. He is the trickster bit of us that is willing to try things and bend the rules.

Tricksters are shapeshifters, self-centered, unconventional, and praxis-oriented. They know through instinct. They are all about the *doing*. Tricksters steal, lie, and violate social conventions. They use whatever means are available in a fashion entirely unconcerned with boundaries. Scruples aren't the fox's concern. But if you need a bit of playfulness or underhandedness, if you need to nose your way into new territory – the fox is your guide.

To take possession of the Blue Falcon, the prince will need to steal it. The prince, a young, naïve, innocent character, has not yet integrated these traits. He has lived by his father's rules in his father's kingdom, so he will need to soften his upright principles for this quest.

By setting out on his quest, even if he is lost and somewhat directionless at this point, the prince is engaging himself and opening himself. But by his engagement he is also inviting the fox to enter in. He is showing his openness to trying things in a new way. At this point in the story, he must use his existing skills to carry out the quest. It is only by doing this that he will gain the additional skills needed to be able to complete the quest.

It is only by taking risks and entering the wider arena of our lives – by becoming visible – that we can evolve and grow. This is not a story of how the prince came up with a new way to organize his suits while never leaving his bedroom. This is a story of how the prince leaves behind all that is comfortable (albeit with a bit of a nasty push) in order to claim a life that will make him proud and use all of who he is.

Just as Eve ate of the apple and that propelled her out of the Garden of Eden, Prince Iain will need to expand his worldview to include the darker aspects of the human heart. Previous beliefs, values, and habits will need to be boiled down until only the fundamentals – the bones – are left.

And that is exactly what the fox offers to share for their dinner: sheep bones boiled over a fire. Fire used in cooking acts as the catalyst for transformation or refinement. Indeed, the prince is gradually leaving his young, naïve self behind as a new self emerges. Bones are the parts of living beings that remain after death. By entering the forest and being on the threshold of changing how he lives his life, the prince is committing to a kind of death. The marrow of bones is said to embody the essence. Here, the marrow and bones – the essence and being of the prince – are being alchemically transformed so they can be taken in and used in a different way.

Sheep are considered passive and meek livestock, easily frightened. As their bones are repeatedly cooked, in the same fashion, the essence of the prince is being transformed in the heat of his quest from naïvety to maturity. He is learning to take the reins of his life.

As we experiment with bending our safe, original paradigm's boundaries, we get to the bones of who we really are. We can discern the elements that were not imposed upon us, but that are authentically important and integral to who we are.

Using fire, we transform tough, inedible, sometimes toxic vegetables and meat into palatable, chewable food. We go through a similar cooking and alchemy to allow our own new self to emerge.

The prince and the fox dine on sheep, transforming passive energy into more active energy that the prince can carry on his journey of learning how to take the reins of his life.

We don't just throw away all past learning and experience. We redeploy the energy and wisdom we've already gained. We reorient to the wider perspective we've gained. In the words of transpersonal psychotherapist Ken Wilber, we transcend and include.

This isn't the last time we'll meet the fox in this tale. There is more of him to come.

First, the prince travels to the house of a five-headed giant. The giant is male, which denotes an overload of archetypal masculine qualities – logic, achievement, linear thought, structure, control, and external ambitions. Put that together with his five heads and we are staring into ten eyes of over-weaned rationality and intellect not connected to feminine principles of spiritual insight and contemplation. In the same way the prince needs to integrate the masculine, so we often need to overcome the over-reliance on cold rationality that our post-industrial society relies on.

We rationalize about why we need to stay in a bad situation. We demean our feelings and numb our yearnings by over-intellectualizing why we must continue as we always have. Although we remain in the house of the giant, when we over-rationalize, we are removed and above a situation. Before damning this entirely, it's good to make use of this. It's not such bad advice to dwell in the giant's house for a while. Learn his ways. Spend some time seeing things objectively. Living here also gives us a good bird's-eye view of where we've come from, as well as a calm place to stand while we catch a glimpse of what may lie ahead.

The giant wants the Sword of Light. Swords are used as weapons and can also stand for discernment. They denote courage, honor, and strength. Some part of the giant knows he needs a sense of discernment to temper his five heads's worth of cold rationality.

Now Iain, though he has not succeeded in capturing the Blue Falcon, knows what his next step is. He would not have known this without having left his known kingdom and having become visible and vulnerable outside of its gates.

Giants and Swords

The dejected prince left the giant's house and went back into the wasteland, where he again came upon Gillie Martin the Fox, who was full of mirth at Iain's situation. He laughed and said, "You're the picture of misery this evening, Prince Iain. All I have to eat is a sheep's leg and jaw, but I'll share what I have with you." So they lit a fire and ate and then slept on the ground.

In the morning, Gillie Martin again offered his advice and assistance. "Together we will journey to the ocean's edge. I will turn myself into a boat to deliver you to Jura. When we get to where the Seven Big Women of Jura live, you will offer to be at their service. Tell them you can polish silver, iron, copper, and gold. If you do everything well, they may trust you with the White Sword of Light. Then, when they are away, you can run off with it. But take care – do not let the sheath touch anything in their house."

They walked all day and got to shore, where, with a great whoosh, the fox turned himself into a sailboat. Prince Iain climbed aboard and they sailed together toward the lush green mountains and the Seven Big Women of Jura. After a long walk from Jura's shore, Iain knocked on the door of the Seven Big Women.

The door opened. "What are you looking for?," the Seven Big Women asked in unison, all jockeying for a place at the door from which to inspect their odd young visitor.

"I'm looking for work," said Iain. "I can polish all metals until they glow like the brightest of moons."

"We need a boy like this," they boomed. And so Iain made his home with them and began polishing all the metal in their home until they grew to rely on him so much that they entrusted him with the White Sword of Light.

When the Seven Big Women of Jura were finally all out at once, Prince Iain sheathed the sword and headed straight for the door. Just as he reached the doorway, however, the sheath scraped against the door, which let out a loud screech! and the Seven Big Women of Jura came thundering home to wrench the White Sword of Light out of Prince Iain's hands.

Squishing from foot to foot in his wet shoes, the prince persuaded them to make a deal. "We will not give you this sword unless you bring to us the Golden Filly of the King of Erin."

Over-Entrenchment and Freedom

Whereas the house of a giant male with five heads denotes an excess of masculine intellectualization, a house of seven large women denotes an excess of feminine energy. Here we are in a place where archetypal feminine qualities rule – passion, instinct, feeling, connection, spontaneity, and sensual appetites. These are arguably what give us our individual sense of meaning.

Sometimes we need to pendulum between these two places – the cold intellectualization and the passionate feeling-led poles – before we can move to the next stage of a quest. Because human beings are both intellectual and sensual, our memories and the feelings associated with our experiences are gathered through this fused combination of stances. This swing between rationality and yearning causes the small revolutions of action required to make the journey of a quest.

By allowing the rational and feeling functions to work independently we can see our surroundings from a detached place. We can dispassionately take in the history and temperaments of the people involved in a situation, and then use our feelings and sensual qualities to discern meaning, such as who we are in relation to others and in what way we need to show up.

Eventually, the two clashing sides wear down the sharp edges of each other and a middle path becomes visible.

In the house of the Seven Big Women, Iain is tasked to work at polishing all sorts of metal. Metal is made from elements pulled from below the earth and then formed into something useful in the world above ground. During our quest, this is what we are doing – pulling attributes and strengths up from our subconscious to be of use in our outer life.

The particular sword of great value here in this story is made of white light. Archetypally, white light can symbolize enlightenment and consciousness.

Again, the prince is unable to make a smooth getaway with his plunder, and this time he is sent to retrieve the Golden Filly from the King of Erin. The young female horse is a symbol for the instinctual power of freedom and independence. Just as the Giant with Five Heads is asking for a balancing item for the masculine intellectual forces, so the Seven Women of Jura are looking for a balance to their overweening feminine attributes.

Prince Iain keeps getting caught at the threshold.

We tend to travel back and forth before committing and belonging to a new place. There is a doorway, a passageway, but it, in and of itself, is also a place. We can pass slightly through and then slightly back. This liminality offers us a place out of time, away from status. Here, we experience emptiness, neutrality, and openness. Who we are and the reality we perceive is suspended. In liminality, we find doorways that allow us respite from the swinging pendulum's limited reach of two opposite dimensions. Here, we can temporarily forget the greater world.

Liminality is where transformation takes place – where things that seemed impossible gain credibility. Elusive elements from our subconscious are brought out and made conscious. This is where we tune in to what our soul is calling for – who we are beyond our history and accustomed roles.

Yet another of the prince's thefts ends in a triggered alarm. And so we may begin to believe that, quite apart from the dashing young hunter he originally appeared to be, the prince is perhaps a clumsy oaf who can't seem to get it right. Over and over, he falls into this same trap.

In our own lives, as well – and with increasing exasperation – we may revisit the same stupid mistakes over and over, until we despair of breaking the pattern.

We, too, get a glimpse of the Blue Falcon, only to miss when we aim for it and then lose sight of it altogether. We fumble with the tools, weapons, and prizes that seem necessary for life and find that what we most need is to cultivate various facets of ourselves – the tedious as well as the interesting – if we are to reach and take the reins of our lives.

We need to prove to ourselves that we are worthy – and that what we seek is possible to achieve. And so we rock back and forth on the threshold of our longed-for world before fully committing to it.

Risk and engagement are always found together. An insight not engaged is lost.

So let the trickster sit at your table. Let him have his say. Take other people's counsel, but use discernment. Do not thuggishly march forward, but dance. We already hold the wide world within us. Whichever aspects of ourselves we do not give a seat to at the banquet table will become the entity we will continually do battle with.

Tricksters help mete out that shadow self we cannot always look at directly. They are amoral rather than immoral – for them, good and evil are intertwined, even undifferentiated. Your trickster aspect gives you a chance to experiment to see which elements you want to fully integrate, which elements you would like to cultivate for specific uses, and which elements you may be willing to acknowledge but not bring out. Lingering for a little while in the threshold allows you to play with those elements, to try them on for size and feel your way toward what feels better.

Integrating one's shadow qualities means finding a safe place to dance with them so that you can reflect back their strengths and integrate them. As you integrate your shadow, you enter into a more authentic relationship with yourself and with the world.

To integrate shadow, we need to know it, and we can only come to know something by engaging with it. As you engage, keep in mind that the trickster can give brilliant advice, or get you into deep trouble. You've got to put his advice into action to find out if you've been handed the keys to the kingdom or been royally set up.

Certainly, for the prince, at this point, and despite trying to follow the fox's advice, he continually sets off alarms, which prompt the angry owners of the things he tries to take. They then require him to retrieve something else the prince never bargained on needing in the first place.

Kings and Independence

Crestfallen, Prince Iain again goes back out into the waste-lands empty-handed.

That evening, he was found by an amused Gillie Martin the Fox, who said, "You're the picture of misery this evening, Prince Iain. All I have to eat is a sheep's leg and jaw, but I'll share what I have with you."

They roasted the bones and mutton over a fire and slept.

In the morning, Gillie Martin said, "I'll shape-shift myself into a grand sailing vessel, complete with three many-sailed masts, and take you to Erin. When you gain an audience with the king, offer to serve as his stable boy. Tell him you can feed and groom the horses, and care for their harnesses and trappings. Keep the horses in good order and the king may trust you with his golden filly. Be sure, when you lead her out of the stable, that no part of her touches any part of the stable gate." Prince Iain nodded and the fox changed into a sailing vessel, and off they sailed, in grand fashion, to Erin.

In Erin, Prince Iain was taken to the king, who accepted his offer of work as a stable boy. In time, Iain was trusted with the care of the golden filly. Everyone in the kingdom could see how well the filly fared under the ministrations of the newest stable boy. Her coat shone, her speed had improved, and her eyes were bright.

And so, one day, the king left the filly in Iain's care when he went out hunting. As Iain led the Golden Filly out, her tail swished ever so slightly against the stable's door-frame, which let out a loud screech! The king came galloping home from the hunt. He was angry, but he offered Iain an option. "Unless you can convince the red-haired daughter of the king of France to be my wife, I will never give you the Golden Filly."

Letting Go to Let Come

Just as the prince in this story returns to the woods between botched attempts to capture the falcon, we visit a transpersonal place between each revolution in the process of change. This is a place where new information and lessons from the chapter we've just externally lived can be brought in and allowed to dance with the internal psyche – to reform and plot for the next step.

If this isn't done, lessons could be lost, or this step could calcify into yet another stuck waystation. Once again, there is a paradox. Although this next step will be slightly different from the last step, we need the time and space for the previous experience to be crystallized and dissolved through inner dialogue.

The connection between the outer, action-oriented world we share with others and the internal, emotional, and personal world – and the transactions that take place in this in-between place – is rarely spoken of.

This phase of the quest is about not wanting to show our hand too soon. Our wavering thoughts and opinions are easily swayed. As our inner voice is developing, we need quiet solitude to hear its soft call and to give it time to gain strength before it strides into the conflictual outer world, strong enough to stand its ground in the face of opposing opinions.

Once we have accepted paradox – that something can be both good and bad, light and dark, kind and savage, all at once – the rocking between our rational mind and our body, intuition, and feelings can abate to stillness.

Within this stillness we become more in touch with our own inner compass. We could even say that it is here that we best hear our soul speak. And the message of our soul may very well take us off our charts and into unknown waters.

Our inner compass recognizes that the world is much larger than our conscious maps indicate. We may not be able to draw further sections of the map yet, but a functioning compass will urge us off the edge, will insistently suggest, and even promise, that there are realms to be visited if you would just push off in a new direction.

Of course, once the newly hatched self leaves the safety and seclusion of our internal landscape, it runs the risk of being mowed down by the dominating cultural imperatives. As J.R.R. Tolkien wrote during the time when the publication of *The Lord of the Rings* was pending, "...it will be impossible not to mind what is said. I have exposed my heart to be shot at."

The inner self must be strong enough to take part in social conventions without being engulfed by them. This is the risk. We fear having this lovely notion we've cultivated and become emotionally attached to let out, only to find that it is, after all, neither viable nor valued.

Risk-taking imparts momentum to life. Through the revolutions of smaller risks, play, intermediate forms of next steps, and repeated visits to our liminal spaces, we cultivate the strength, adaptability, and resilience needed to take the larger risks. Through those revolutions, we also gain the ability to discern the superfluous from the vital and let go of the superfluous. This discernment comes more from strengthening the inner compass than from an external dependence on validation.

৩৫৩

The prince's next stop is the palace of a king. This king, this person, is human-sized instead of giant, which immediately makes him more approachable than the previous overlords Prince Iain has worked for. We are closing in on balance. Although the king isn't willing to hand the prince what he needs, this more balanced figure becomes the penultimate character that sends the prince in a direction that will lead to his triumphant return home.

The king in this story represents the balanced intelligence that comes out of the dialogue between inner world and outer that can take place in the in-between place. The king points the prince in what turns out to be the right direction to turn his luck around. Just so, this type of intelligence can inform us and give us a much clearer and encompassing view as it integrates rational and instinctual dimensions. But then we must put the wise mission we've received into action.

This is where the risk to bring our inner life and outer world into alignment begins to be needed in earnest.

Prince Iain sets to work grooming the horses and the filly – symbolically improving his ability to be independent and claim his independence, to have the strength to see his intentions through.

Intentions take form as our sense of primary inner directedness and our locus of evaluation moves from outside to inside. External validators are replaced with internal validators. Only with a sense of personal centeredness can we encounter "the other" without being washed away.

Through engagement and playing, we form an intermediate self, a trial way of being. These temporary, in-between forms of ourselves are loosely formed and easy to dissipate and reform into slightly different beings. Like Prince Iain, who had to set out on his quest before he could get as far as the balanced king, we, too, must begin before we know what we will find.

The king of Erin is looking for a wife. Again we see that this character is seeking balance. The prince sets sail from his homeland and crosses the sea to France to lure a princess onto his ship. The foreignness of the other country denotes Prince Iain's full entry into another paradigm. Here is the point of risk. He must leave sight of his known land and fully commit to this course. Setting sail to France is a leap of faith. He has no guarantee that his ship will survive the journey, or that the princess will come back with him.

To take big risks we need to let go – not only of shorelines, relationships, or jobs – but of addictions, anger, mindsets, and "shoulds." The relinquishment of these aspects is crucial to allowing a leap of faith. Along Prince Iain's journey, he has approached this threshold a few times. Not quite making it over builds a foundation from which he can take a risk to launch himself. And so it is for us as we gather the inner strength to launch ourselves.

Only by letting go may we let the next growth come. Without letting go, we leave no space for other things, new things, to grow. Letting go entails a form of destruction.

The old way often makes excellent compost for what is to come.

Foreign Princess and Returning to Claim the Kingdom

And so, again, Prince Iain left empty-handed. He found Gillie Martin sniggering at him by the seaside. "Ah, Iain. You look the picture of misery. Come. I'll turn myself into a ship again and we'll get you to France in no time."

Across the channel they sailed, until they reached the shore of France, where Gillie Martin the Fox, as boat, grounded them upon the rocks of the shore. There Iain climbed down to the seashore where the king of France, his queen, and their red-haired daughter were spending the day.

"Where have you come from and what are you doing here?" asked the king.

"Our ship lost its bearings and we have run aground on your rocks, sir," said Iain. "I'm not sure we'll be able to get her off to sea again."

Just then a beautiful and eerie music began playing from deep within the ship. The red-haired princess was filled with curiosity and climbed aboard looking for the source of the sound. Prince Iain followed her onto the boat. The music seemed to be coming from cabins in the lowest portion of the boat, but each time the princess felt she was reaching it, the sound moved further away. Iain smiled, watching her graceful and inquisitive face move from level to level until they had walked from the lowest cabins and reached again the top deck.

The princess gasped to see that, by this time, they were far out to sea. "You've played a terrible trick on me," she said, turning on Iain. "Where are you taking me?"

Prince Iain bowed his head. "We are sailing to Erin, where the king waits for you. He will then give me his Golden Filly, which I will give to the Seven Big Women of Jura in return for the White Sword of Light, which I'll give to the Brutish Giant with Five Heads in return for the Blue Falcon, which I will give to my evil stepmother so that she'll free me from her curse. You will be safe with the King of Erin, for he has heard of your beauty and wishes to make you his wife."

"I'd rather be your wife," said the red-haired princess of France. Prince Iain felt a strong wave of agreement.

When they docked in Erin, Gillie Martin turned himself into a woman as beautiful as the princess of France and Prince Iain presented him to the king of Erin, who gladly gave over the Golden Filly, so besotted was he with his new companion. Iain got on the filly and galloped back to the red-haired princess, who was waiting by the seashore. When the king of Erin and his new wife went to bed, Gillie Martin tore a great gash into the King's chest and ran straight down to the sea again.

Next, they sailed to Jura. The fox shape-shifted to appear as the Golden Filly, which Prince Iain saddled and delivered to the Seven Big Women. Thrilled with the horse, the Seven Big Women gave Iain the White Sword of Light. They then formed a gigantic totem and sat atop each other, shoulders on hips, shoulders on hips, all seven Big Women tall on the back of the Golden Filly. They whacked it with a stick and it took off running over the moors and up to the top of the highest mountain. There on the edge of a steep precipice, the filly kicked up its legs and the Seven Big Women of Jura were thrown over the cliff. Gillie Martin shifted back into himself and ran back to the prince, the red-haired princess, the Golden Filly, and the White Sword of Light.

Gillie-as-boat then sailed them across the water to the mainland, where he turned himself into the White Sword of Light. Prince Iain carried him to the Brutish Giant with Five Heads who, in return, gave him the Blue Falcon nestled into its basket. The Giant began swinging the sword in giant arcs, fencing with his shadow. Suddenly, the sword became very unwieldy and – just as you could almost make out the form of a fox from within the light – the sword turned and swiped off all five heads of the Brutish Giant.

Now, at last, the prince was ready to return to his father's castle and deal with the evil queen.

At the castle walls, Gillie Martin instructed Iain to ride the Golden Filly with the red-haired princess behind him, holding the basket with the Blue Falcon in it. Most importantly, the fox said, he was to hold the White Sword of Light so the sharp side of sword faced his stepmother and hold the other edge against his nose. If he failed in this, Gillie Martin said, the evil queen would turn him into a pile of firewood.

Prince Iain was especially careful and did exactly as the fox instructed. As he neared his very wet and windblown step-

mother she glared a curse upon him which hit the White Sword of Light and glanced back upon her, collapsing her into a pile of sticks which then burned to ash.

Prince Iain had done it. He now had the most marvelous wife in Scotland, the fast and beautiful Golden Filly, the Blue Falcon to keep him supplied with game from the forest, and the White Sword of Light to defend him from enemies.

Prince Iain invited the fox to live with him and his wife and promised him a good and prosperous life now that he would soon be crowned king. Gillie Martin, not to be kept, blessed the prince and his princess and went on his way.

Letting Go to Let Come

Once grounded upon the shore of France, Iain enchants the princess onto the boat with music. Her boarding of the boat means she is now present in the prince's world. As she explores to find the music, she progresses to deeper and deeper cabins – realms of the subconscious.

The prince is no longer collecting tools for others or following orders. He's using the available tools to his own advantage.

But the trickster fox is still at the helm.

The princess has red hair. In archetypal terms, red represents rebelliousness and visceral life force. Indeed, the princess who has accepted that she has been stolen away does not assent to marry the king of Erin. When she tells Prince Iain, "I would rather marry you," balance is achieved. Insight and action are together.

The red-haired princess knows herself. She brings a more ordered and centered feminine energy than the outmoded evil stepmother who lashes out and does not guide. This new feminine aspect supports and informs rather than maliciously strikes out.

Together, she and the prince will defy old paradigms.

Now all tools and elements have been gathered. It's time to go back and claim the rightful kingdom – the self. Things move along more smoothly now, as outer characters – light and dark – become more integrated.

The monsters are dispatched. The giants, the monsters, represent overblown and unbalanced parts of the psyche, and they will now disappear as balance is brought in. Monsters – representing addictions, bad habits, overgrown, unbalanced, and destructive parts of the self that no longer work – are being cut away.

The prince returns home to claim his kingdom. Can you imagine him claiming the castle and kingdom before taking that journey, before mastering the tools in his armory, without the belief in himself that came from the trials he faced, or without the new queen and the intuitive balance she brought?

The big leap that Prince Iain could not have achieved earlier is now only a step away.

We sense it happening when all things come together in a moment – mind, body, emotions – all aspects converging.

Of course, when the newly hatched self leaves the safety and seclusion of our internal landscape, it runs the risk of being mowed down by the dominating cultural imperatives. This is the risk. We fear having this lovely notion we've cultivated, and become emotionally attached to, let out only to find that it is, after all, neither viable nor valued. The prince, and we, need to have gone through the test runs and made mistakes and tweaked our approach, in order to feel we have gained enough strength to finally see this large risk through. We need to have gone through the earlier rotations to stand up strongly for our resolution, even – and especially in the face of – others's disagreement. We need to have grown strong enough, which is only possible through trying, adapting, refocusing, trying again.

This cohesive drive at the center of our beings is that golden ball from the Frog Prince and the culmination of the risk we took when we left the Garden of Eden, the safe but enclosed place from which we grew.

The world has not changed, but our field of vision has expanded – taking in the array and permutations of possible outcomes and ways to handle potential eventualities. Our skills –psychological and practical – have been cultivated and established.

These periods of letting go and reconstitution have built up our stamina for enduring discomfort. The revolutions have given us a sense of mastery over our lives, as well as strength. The ability to take fundamental risks rests on the culmination of an emerging gestalt that we have journeyed far to bring to a conclusion. We have learned how to take the reins of our own life. We trust in our abilities and step out of our invisibility.

જ્જ

The princess falls in love with the prince and they return to rule his kingdom. When the princess takes residence in the castle, the external and internal worlds are in union again. The new king (outer world) and new queen (inner world) are now able to communicate. They know each other as their true selves. There is balance and accord between passion and rationality.

This balance, and the intercourse between inner and outer worlds, is only one of the collateral blessings of risk. Just as the prince returns with much more than the Blue Falcon he set out to capture – we gain a better understanding of ourselves. We gain discernment, wisdom, resilience, faith, courage, compassion, freedom, and a sense of purpose.

But also, importantly, there is a sense of *balance* between the external and the internal elements, and that gives us wisdom. We are connected *to our inner compass*. We are more tuned in to our own voice. Blind principles are now pointed out by the soul's voice. The principles that loosened during the phase of risk-taking have likely returned – but are now deployed differently. Because of this, we are more grounded and authentic with ourselves, so we have more authentic relationships with others.

Paradoxically, the more one is able to be flexible regarding reactions and acceptance, the more solid, focused, and ever-present our own souls become. A connection to our inner voice leads us to our purpose and gives us resilience. Resilience is the ability to spring back into shape after being pressed or stretched. It is the ability to recover strength, spirits, good humor, or any other aspect quickly. Resilience allows us to adapt and to improvise in unknown situations.

Resilience is a result of engagement, particularly engagement in which difficulties are weathered. Although fear remains when we take risks, after testing ourselves with risk, the faith begins to outweigh the fear.

When you put resilience and faith together, courage is cultivated. Courage is obtained from testing and coming to know not only our strengths and limits, but also to know that after we've broken a limit – even if we've failed – we will regroup and carry on.

When we are committed to an action from the level of our soul, we are willing to take risks in service of that action. Our inner voice speaks what is deeply meaningful to us and we listen. Courage comes naturally when our heart is behind an action.

In a cascade effect, resilience, faith, and courage come together to become freedom. Through risks and engagement, in a process that was clumsy at first, the prince becomes worthy of the confidence and abilities that allow him to rule his own kingdom. The Blue Falcon, once possessed, becomes an integral part of the kingdom, as opposed to the be-all and end-all that the prince's comfort hinges on.

We hold up roles and labels as shields: wife, mother. We think of ourselves as having a place and an accepted value. As we move on, we slowly lose or choose to dissolve the roles and shields that once were a sort of shorthand for our value, an accepted garment that felt natural and comfortable. We become visible, able to be seen more as ourselves than as our role.

This can feel so very vulnerable.

Perhaps what we experience now as a destination reached, an obstacle overcome, is, in fact, only the latest in a series of small revolutions, one that will be eclipsed by another revolution down the line. We will only be able to reach that point by taking the step we are on the verge of taking now.

We don't give back the self-confidence, skills, sense of freedom, ability to hear our inner voice, or accomplished sensation of moving through difficulty. They have been somatized and have become part of our body and our heart. They cultivate and nourish our soul, feed our mind, and inform us of who we are.

Our kingdom just grew a lot bigger.

As our world becomes increasingly interconnected through globalization, challenges to personal paradigms are set to increase in quantity as well as intensity. Blue feathers and unsettling paradigm "cracks" are inevitable.

A global culture will always be dynamic and filled with paradox, but if we can embrace our ability to retain the essence of who we are, yet also be fluid enough to interact with and be touched by others, we can embrace adaptability and reflexivity – skills which are surely becoming ever more crucial.

When Prince Iain returns home holding the Sword of Light up against his face, the newfound consciousness that he has integrated casts away the evil. Just as the other monsters disappeared and were killed off when balance was brought in, so, too, must the stepmother go. From our state of balance and insight, we see what is coming and can defend or annihilate threats as needed. We recognize evil for what it is and now have the tools and knowledge to deal with it. We are no longer suddenly overtaken and forced to its will. We can choose.

The evil stepmother has been taken from the outside and has been integrated into the prince's new kingdom, in the form of his princess bride. The feminine no longer needs to exist outside, as the enemy.

Prince Iain has lived outside and engaged outside in the world. He has learned from the trickster fox and is not so innocent anymore. He is ready to rule his kingdom, along with his new wife – the balancing feminine.

Before his adventure, led by the clever, crafty fox (a shadow figure), the prince had been a paragon of virtue – all light, no darkness or shadow – and, as such, was unbalanced and, therefore, not fit to rule a kingdom. We are vulnerable in the outside world to anything we do not know about in ourselves. We can only fight evil in the outer world once we have transcended our own innocence. The world is full of paradoxes and complications that we must learn to accept and exist with. When we integrate our own Sword of Light, we gain powers of discrimination, because our direction is guided by our own North Star.

When we read and interpret myths and fairy tales, what we take from them is our own. The prince achieves success when he no longer gives his inner treasures to others, but deploys them in service to his own soul. He has thus reached adulthood. He has journeyed through the small revolutions necessary to reach the goal: his triumphant return.

Journal Prompts

Feather theme. The blue feather that the prince starts off with is like an urge for a response from the universe. There is very likely a theme, or a strand of a theme, that has dogged you your whole life. Think of this as the universe leaving sticky notes throughout the narrative of your life.

Can you name some recurring sticky notes, or blue feathers, from the universe that have shown up in your life?

Falcon's eyes. See the past through a falcon's eyes. Read your life backward. What were you meant to learn from? What memories are tinged with a traumatic brush and thus have gotten stuck, keeping you from moving on? What strengths have you built up from misfortune? What stealthy gifts have buoyed you along, no matter how you ignored and misaligned with them? What of your characteristics are bullying others into submission?

Visual and Sensory Prompt

Your life has been a long and winding journey, just as the prince's has. Draw a map representing the winding road and beasties you've encountered along the way. What did you learn from each encounter with a monster? What did you need to leave behind to move forward?

Geek Fact

In fairy tales and myths, reigning kings and queens were often replaced by the end with a prince and princess – psychologically, the revivified masculine and feminine energies within us – whose story was just beginning. In ancient history, however, there were many cultures in Africa and Asia that, in actuality, sacrificed kings when they became ill or old.

Conclusion

We claim our kingdom through the journey of claiming our golden ball, honoring our intuitive, growth-centered, deepening into the world, and allowing ourselves to walk our soul's journey – despite the absurdities and divine stumbles along the way.

We break the spell of invisibility by *allowing* ourselves to be visible in the world. When we bring our soul's light into the world, we attract people who are looking for the tribe that is also ours.

When you do this, you become a woman in possession of herself and her power. You become creative, connected to spirit and community. Powerful. Kind. Beautiful. Magical. You allow yourself to have a sensual experience – living in balance with your soul – that enriches you and brings you into your own luscious journey. You build confidence, certainty, and honor for your soul's mission. You feel that you are a part of life, not at odds with it. You feel that you are a vital part of life, worthy and essential. You claim a connection to the underground, to your inner life.

There comes a point, somewhere during the middle of our lives, when we need to take responsibility for the things that happen to us. In J. K. Rowling's brilliant commencement address to a Harvard graduating class, she announced that, "There is an expiry date on blaming your parents...." This also applies to ex-husbands, crummy circumstances, and apocalyptically misguided decisions of our own.

Perhaps a sense of having lived in this world, and lived well, rests more on the trials and painful initiations that birth us into our wholeness than on the days of cake and sunshine.

ᔕᕈᑎ

I'll conclude this book with one more story, a short one.

This story is about a master archer who keeps looking for others to teach him more, for guidance from outside himself, even though he has already met and surpassed the skills of all the archers he has found. He wanted to remain ever in the role of student and devotee rather than risk assuming master in the open field of life.

Yes, we always have more to learn, but there comes a time when learning must evolve from theoretical scriptures delivered from podiums – into actual trial and error, play and replay, in the real world.

The Archer

Once upon a time, in a village set in the mountains, there lived an archer. He had surpassed all of his teachers in accuracy, rate of fire, ability to shoot from unusual positions, and much more. Still, he was convinced there was another teacher somewhere with yet more for him to learn, so he set off on a quest to find them.

From village to village he travelled, but he could find no archers who could best him in skill. A full year later, as he wandered along the forest paths in the remotest reaches of the kingdom, he found an arrow stuck in a tree directly in the center of a painted target.

He wandered further, and found more and more of these perfectly released arrows that never missed their mark. Within the rag-tag countryside, he saw yet more arrows in targets – on sides of barns, hen houses, and signposts.

The archer knew he had found his new master, but where did the great man live? He began asking everyone he passed where he might find this skilled archer. No one knew of whom he spoke.

He persevered, asking wise men in the local village, woodcutters, farmers, milkmaids, children – and still no one knew of a master archer who lived in the area. In a state of frustrated despair, he sat down on a log deep in the forest. There, in that quiet space, he could just detect the scent of a fire burning, and he looked up and around until he saw little wisps of smoke rising through the trees.

He followed the scent of the smoke until he reached a ramshackle house with a scrawny goat tied up just outside it, and an old woman inside. The archer bowed his head and told the old woman of his quest and asked if she knew of this skilled marksman who had populated the area with perfectly hit targets – never a miss or even so much as deviation of an inch away from dead center.

"Ahhhh." The old woman smiled. She led the seeking archer to a glade and said, "Sit here on this log tomorrow as the sun is going down. Here you will meet your master archer."

The next day, the archer quietly sat on the log, excitedly anticipating the arrival of a great master. Just as the last rays of sun were disappearing behind the treetops he heard light footsteps approaching. Amidst the trees he saw a young girl with a quiver of arrows and a satchel. He watched her place her satchel on the ground and pull an arrow out of her quiver, pull it back taut, and let it fly. The arrow wedged into an oak that stood only several steps away from her, so the arrow had bit deeply into the bark.

Then she leaned down to open her satchel and pulled out a small pot and a brush.

Around her arrow, she painted a perfect circle with the tip of the arrow in the exact center.

The archer has learned enough. Now he will take what he knows and put it into practice to make a life of his experiences and skills without continuing to check his own abilities against others to see if he is doing better or more; without trying to perfect further what is already honed.

It's time to expand himself and take on new challenges. It's time to learn something new.

Your arrows will find their way. Let them hit where they will and let others choose what about that is important and what is not. I promise you they will anyway, whether you are speaking your own truth, or running with someone else's.

We need to have the courage of our convictions and experience, and share them, so that those walking in our path may learn, just as we have learned from those who have gone before us.

This is what is so magical about therapy – we look for answers within ourselves. In doing so and also in living in the world, we engage in a co-creation of society and ourselves. We are here, in this space and time, to dance our dance... in the communities in which we live.

What if we believed in ourselves, in the truths inside us, in the emerging voice that persists – no matter the pushback in front of us? The trick is in choosing how to express our truth, not by rewriting it or in mangling ourselves, but by finding the most graceful and creative way to show up, nonetheless.

What in these stories has resonated in your soul? What parts of you have been moved as you've read them and pondered their depths beyond their surface layer of words?

సౌ

I would love to hear more about your experiences and thoughts. I invite you to contact me at

www.wendy-hammond.com.

I wish you much love and deep, soulful living.

ACKNOWLEDGEMENTS

Thank you to my editor, Grace Kerina, who has again encouraged and corralled my thoughts to form a cohesive book rather than a disjointed collection of interesting points. Also, a thank you to Angela Lauria, publisher extraordinaire, whose straightforward manner and clever coaching are forces to be reckoned with.

Thank you to Neil Cameron, whose intelligence and general brilliance are precious to me. He is an excellent crisis-point wordsmith and best friend.

Thank you to my friends and family, who are guiding lights and fun allies. Special shout-outs to Betsy Pearson, Lynn Poulos, Emily Downward, Caroline Greengrow, and Vanessa Lee – who especially inspired and encouraged me during the writing of this book, and to my sisters, Heather and Megan, and their beautiful families.

Thank you to Kim Hermanson, an excellent facilitator of creativity and a power-of-metaphor ninja. Our phone calls have kept me on course and in flow during this process. And thanks also to Marie Yu, brilliant hypnotherapist.

Thank you to my progeny, who have independently walked dogs and created meals during the writing of this book, which made life in this house infinitely freer. I'm so grateful.

And thanks to my clients, whose courage and openness inspire me daily. Thank you for honoring with me with your confidences and allowing me to be witness to your transformations.

I'm wildly grateful to you all.

ABOUT THE
AUTHOR

Wendy Hammond helps people expand past false limits in their personal narratives. She uses cognitive approaches to help her clients call forth their creative imagination, nurture their confidence, and strengthen their sense of meaning. As an author, psychotherapist, and coach, she uses the power of metaphor from dreams, art, myth, and nature to illuminate guiding patterns in our lives. Her clinical practice has focused on life's transitional periods, and the infinite forms transformations take.

Wendy is mom to three wonderful teenagers and two dogs. Her own childhood was spent catching frogs and wandering the woods and grape vineyards near Lake Erie. Since then, she has lived and worked in New York, Tokyo, Hong Kong, and London, and is now in Philadelphia. Always, she has been a great lover of tapping in to mythology and fairy tales as a way to explore mind-sets and cultures from the inside out.

Wendy's favorite speaking topic is the intersection between our internal lives today and the stories that have captivated humanity's attention since pre-history.

About Difference Press

Difference Press offers entrepreneurs, including life coaches, healers, consultants, and community leaders, a comprehensive solution to get their books written, published, and promoted. A boutique-style alternative to self-publishing, Difference Press boasts a fair and easy-to-understand profit structure, low-priced author copies, and author-friendly contract terms. Its founder, Dr. Angela Lauria, has been bringing to life the literary ventures of hundreds of authors-in-transformation since 1994.

Let's Make A Difference With Your Book

You've seen other people make a difference with a book. Now it's your turn. If you are ready to stop watching and start taking massive action, reach out.

"Yes, I'm ready!"

In a market where hundreds of thousands books are published every year and are never heard from again, all participants of The Author Incubator have bestsellers that are actively changing lives and making a difference.

In two years we've created over 174 bestselling books in a row, 90% from first-time authors. We do this by selecting the highest quality and highest potential applicants for our future programs.

Our program doesn't just teach you how to write a book - our team of coaches, developmental editors, copy editors, art directors, and marketing experts incubate you from book idea to published bestseller, ensuring that the book you create can actually make a difference in the world. Then we give you the training you need to use your book to make the difference you want to make in the world, or to create a business out of serving your readers.

If you have life- or world-changing ideas or services, a servant's heart, and the willingness to do what it REALLY takes to make a difference in the world with your book, go to **http://theauthorincubator.com/apply/** to complete an application for the program today.

OTHER BOOKS BY DIFFERENCE PRESS

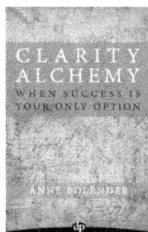

Clarity Alchemy: When Success Is Your Only Option

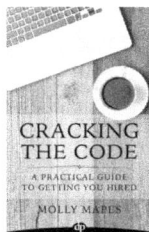

by Ann Bolender

Cracking the Code: A Practical Guide to Getting You Hired

by Molly Mapes

Divorce to Divine: Becoming the Fabulous Person You Were Intended to Be

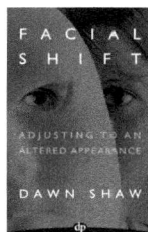

by Cynthia Claire

Facial Shift: Adjusting to an Altered Appearance

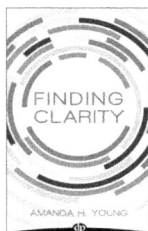

by Dawn Shaw

Finding Clarity: Design a Business You Love and Simplify Your Marketing

by Amanda H. Young

Flourish: Have It All Without Losing Yourself

by Dr. Rachel Talton

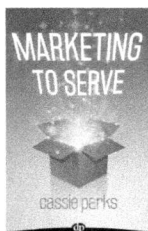

Marketing To Serve: The Entrepreneur's Guide to Marketing to Your Ideal Client and Making Money with Heart and Authenticity

by Cassie Parks

NEXT: How to Start a Successful Business That's Right for You and Your Family

by Caroline Greene

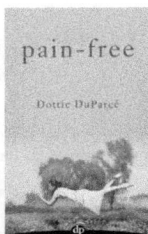

Pain Free: How I Released 43 Years of Chronic Pain

by Dottie DuParcé (Author), John F. Barnes (Foreword)

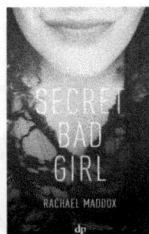

Secret Bad Girl: A Sexual Trauma Memoir and Resolution Guide

by Rachael Maddox

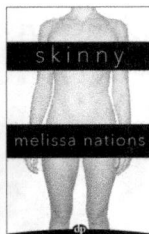

Skinny: The Teen Girl's Guide to Making Choices, Getting the Thin Body You Want, and Having the Confidence You've Always Dreamed Of

by Melissa Nations

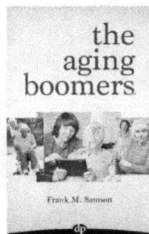

The Aging Boomers: Answers to Critical Questions for You, Your Parents and Loved Ones

by Frank M. Samson

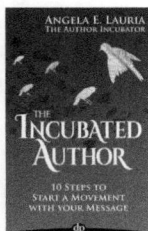

The Incubated Author: 10 Steps to Start a Movement with Your Message

by Angela Lauria

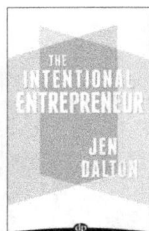

The Intentional Entrepreneur: How to Be a Noisebreaker, Not a Noisemaker

by Jen Dalton (Author), Jeanine Warisse Turner (Foreword)

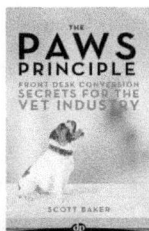

The Paws Principle: Front Desk Conversion Secrets for the Vet Industry

by Scott Baker

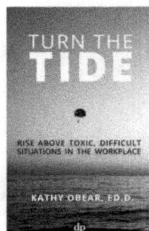

Turn the Tide: Rise Above Toxic, Difficult Situations in the Workplace

by Kathy Obear

THANK YOU

Thank you so much for taking the time to read my book. Please visit me at **www.wendy-hammond.com** to get a free, downloadable workbook to help you illuminate the symbols showing up in your life.

Do email me with dreams or synchronicities that came to you as a response to reading this book.

I wish you very well on your journey.

www.ingramcontent.com/pod-product-compliance
Lightning Source LLC
LaVergne TN
LVHW051350080426
835509LV00020BA/3376